Be Bold!

Be Bold!

Inspiring primary school collective worship

Paulette Bissell, Lisa Fenton, Lizzie McWhirter, Alison Seaman
Edited by Alison Seaman

CHURCH HOUSE PUBLISHING

Church House Publishing
Church House
Great Smith Street
London
SW1P 3NZ
Tel: 020-7898-1451
Fax: 020-7898-1449

ISBN 0 7151 4004 3

Published 2004 by Church House Publishing.

Printed in England by William Clowes Ltd, Beccles, Suffolk

Contents

Introduction

I like the plays and the stories. And I like the sort of worship like we had this morning, where there are lots of candles lit. It just relaxes you before you go into school.

Year Six pupil

In all Anglican schools, worship should reflect the rich traditions of prayer and worship that characterize the worldwide community of Christians. School policy and practice also need to conform to legal requirements concerning worship, in that it must take place every day and should follow the requirements of the Trust Deed. In community schools the requirements for the content of collective worship, while less specific, also necessitate that worship should reflect the broad traditions of Christian belief and be 'wholly or mainly of a broadly Christian character'.

But how can schools move beyond simply complying with legal requirements? How can worship be set in a context that inspires and challenges pupils and offers an opportunity to experience God in 'the beauty of holiness'? How can pupils and staff be given the opportunity to worship together in a way that is enjoyable and spiritually uplifting?

All schools are different in character and setting; distinctive qualities emerge from the mix of individuals and contexts that make up any school community. In 2002, Lord Dearing, in his report to the Archbishops' Council, challenged Anglican schools to be 'sufficiently distinctive in their spiritual life'. School worship is singled out in the report for the significant role it has to play in creating this distinctiveness. It is a challenge that can be taken up by all schools as they mould and nurture the special character and ethos that identify each individual school community. In *Be Bold!* a resource has been created that shows how elements of the Christian tradition can be used for a programme of collective worship that takes seriously the spiritual life of the whole school community.

Be Bold!: Why?

Over the years, the authors of *Be Bold!* have had the privilege of working alongside teachers and worship leaders in schools around the country. In *Be Bold!* they have pooled their knowledge and experience to create a collective worship resource for all schools when planning and presenting acts of worship that reflect the Christian tradition. Aspects of the background materials and the worship resources are aimed specifically at helping Church schools nurture their Christian character and distinctiveness.

The authors' starting point was the questions frequently asked of them by the many headteachers, teachers and worship leaders with whom they work:

How can we be distinctive in our worship?

How can we be explicitly Christian without being oppressive?

How can we be inspirational, rather than institutionalized?

How can we provide a safe atmosphere in which pupils can talk and think freely about God?

The response to these questions seems to point to the need for confidence in celebrating and using the Christian Church's spiritual life and customs; to encourage pupils to engage in a lively and imaginative way with the tradition. It requires a willingness to try new ideas, to take risks, to push at the boundaries of current experience; it requires boldness, and hence the title of this book.

Be Bold! is a resource bank of ideas, inspiration, training materials and visual resources that reflects the Christian faith and, in particular, the Anglican tradition in all its diversity and richness. It is designed to support and encourage confidence in creating and leading a school worship programme.

Be Bold! is a reflective tool for teachers and worship leaders: it contains *ideas* for collective worship; it offers suggestions about creating the *environment* in which to do it; it promotes thinking about the ethos of the *community* in which all this happens.

Be Bold!: The structure

To ensure worship has meaning and purpose demands energy and imagination. Time is always at a premium, so a range of materials have been presented to be used at different times and in different ways. Each chapter follows a similar pattern.

A *Christian symbol*, which can be copied onto an overhead transparency, can be used at any time as a visual focus for any act of worship.

Introducing the theme offers 'food for thought' about the chapter's theme and is of particular support to those in leadership roles and those preparing for a school inspection.

Ways of using the theme is a source of ideas for all teachers and worship leaders. These are suggestions of things to try out and to explore that are simple to implement.

Acts of worship are offered in each chapter to illustrate the theme and as an example to follow through. They are presented as individual acts of worship, but many of them contain enough material to use for a series of acts of worship. Some are designed for the 'big occasions' in the school calendar; others are much simpler in approach. They reflect many different styles of presentation and can easily be adapted to fit different settings and circumstances. Each example has a supporting image that can be copied onto an overhead transparency and used as a focus for the act of worship.

Something to think about forms the final section of each chapter. A framework of questions and discussion-starters has been devised and presented as a photocopiable resource, giving a structure for an INSET session or for a worship planning meeting. It offers a tool for reflection and for action planning.

The final chapter of the book, 'Be Structured', is designed as a tool to help put all this into action; it provides a framework into which all the different ingredients can go. It is a step-by-step guide to developing a shared understanding of collective worship and for planning and implementing a school worship programme. Each of the activities will stand alone, but they can also be followed through in sequence, for example in a worship planning group or staff meeting, for a deeper exploration of collective worship.

Be Bold! has been written mainly with primary schools in mind, but, as with all resource banks, the ideas can be adapted and used in different settings. The background sections and the training materials offered in each chapter have relevance for teachers and worship leaders working at all key stages. If you are looking for some fresh approaches; if you want to revise your worship programme; if you want to inspire colleagues with imaginative ideas, *Be Bold!* is the place to start. There is something of interest in each chapter of *Be Bold!* for every school; for worship coordinators, for headteachers and teachers; for visiting clergy and worship leaders; for school advisers and inspectors.

Be Bold!: The authors

Be Bold! has been written by a team of authors working collaboratively; the reader will hear different voices operating within the structure of the book. This way of working is intended to reflect the diversity of the tradition and the range of experience the authors bring to their work.

Paulette Bissell has taught in primary and secondary schools around the country. She was head of religious studies prior to becoming the Schools Religious Education Adviser for the Diocese of Lincoln. She has been a member of several national working groups supporting religious and spiritual development and values education in schools.

Lisa Fenton was a primary-school teacher until 1998, when she was appointed the Senior Adviser to Schools for Religious Education and Collective Worship in the Diocese of Blackburn. She also lectures at St Martin's College, Lancaster and is a regular contributor to national religious education publications.

Lizzie McWhirter has wide experience of primary-school teaching, having taught for 15 years and lectured in primary religious education before becoming Religious Education, Spirituality and Schools Officer for Coventry Diocese. As an adviser and inspector for Church schools, she has written and researched materials for school worship, religious education and spiritual development. She serves on a number of national RE bodies.

Alison Seaman was for many years a primary school teacher before joining the Church of England's education service as Director of the National Society's Religious Education Centre in London. She is now an education consultant and facilitator of groups wishing to reflect on their educational and working practice. She has written a range of books and support materials for pupils and teachers on religious education and spiritual development.

The book is dedicated to the many pupils and teachers around the country who dare to '**be bold**' in their worship and who inspire others to follow in their footsteps.

Be Bold!: OHT Christian symbol – cross

1. Be Bold!

Introducing the theme

> You are the light of the world. A city on a hill cannot be hidden. No one after lighting a lamp puts it under the bushel basket, but on the lampstand, and it gives light to all in the house. In the same way, let your light shine before others, so that they may see your good works and give glory to your Father in heaven.
>
> *Matthew 5.14-16*

In the Sermon on the Mount, Jesus commands his followers to be light, to give light and to shine so that all may see their good work and praise God. As communities founded upon the Christian faith, and following in the Christian way, Church schools are challenged to respond to this command. Lord Dearing's report on Church schools (*The Way Ahead*, p. 33) recognizes this challenge in its recommendations. It states:

> In all circumstances we would recommend that Church schools must be distinctively places where the Christian faith is alive and practised.

So, how could or should a Church school respond to this challenge? The material in this chapter suggests that the overwhelming response should be with **boldness**. By introducing the challenge in this way, you may feel the approach to be very serious, perhaps like a rather pious duty; a hard, obligatory task. This is certainly not the intention. Rather it is an opportunity to explore that distinctiveness that all Church schools can offer; an opportunity to ensure that the Christian foundation of the school is made clear.

It is very important to stress, before exploring this idea any further, that being bold does not mean to proselytize or indoctrinate. A Church school is not a place where Christian beliefs and values are forced to become part of anyone's life. Rather it is a place where pupils, teachers and parents can witness Christianity in action and be part of a community built around Gospel values. Church schools can be actively involved in the life of the Church and the worldwide Christian community. The school's collective worship provides an excellent opportunity and vehicle for this 'boldness'. When this boldness spreads, and becomes integral to all aspects of school life, it becomes possible to identify it, but impossible to separate it; the school becomes an environment where 'being light' is simply doing what you do.

According to the *Collins English Dictionary* the word '**bold**' is an adjective meaning daring, presumptuous and prominent. Therefore, for a Church school, being bold means to dare to be different, to be confident in the faith it represents and to stand out as a holy place; to be a city on a hill. In the words of the late Lord Runcie, when he was Archbishop of Canterbury, 'Nourish those of the faith; encourage those of other faiths; challenge those who have no faith.'

This chapter explores ways in which Church schools can do just that through collective worship.

Ways of using the theme

Dazzling colour

> I have set my bow in the clouds, and it
> shall be a sign of the covenant between
> me and the earth.
>
> *Genesis 9.13*

In the Book of Genesis, God seals his promise
with a dazzling arch of colour. Can we follow this
example to be bold and colourful? This can be
done very simply by adding a vase of flowers to
the focus table or in a more grand display of
banners hanging in the hall. The use of a focus
table or display boards can add interest and
vibrancy. Pictures, photographs, natural objects,
crosses, icons, books, maps, plants, words,
fabric and balloons are just some examples.
A variety of these resources can be used
throughout the year to bring added colour to
your worship time. Bring Bible stories alive with
bright visual aids, puppets and story sacks. The
visual impact of quality splashes of colour gives
worth and value to the worship.

The sound of silence

> And after the earthquake a fire, but the
> Lord was not in the fire; and after the fire a
> sound of sheer silence. When Elijah heard
> it, he . . . went out and stood at the
> entrance of the cave.
>
> *1 Kings 19.12-13*

When challenged to be bold perhaps our first
reaction is to be loud and very active. From this
account of Elijah's encounter with God we can
learn that sometimes the best way is through
quietness. Pupils are frequently asked to be quiet
but only rarely given time to explore the quiet or
become comfortable with the power of silence.
The introduction of quiet times adds a new
dimension to the experience of worship.

Lighting candles, playing soft music or telling
a story using a gentle voice helps to build
atmosphere. A pause for reflection on the
meaning of a story or the opportunity for
pupils to say silent prayers can deepen their
understanding of themselves and of God.

A clear voice

> Remove the sandals from your feet, for the place on which you
> are standing is holy ground.
>
> *Exodus 3.5*

In this conversation, recorded in the Book of Exodus, God called to
Moses in a clear voice with a clear message. Ensure that the worship
leader speaks clearly and can be heard. Use several members of staff
and outside speakers to lead worship, so that a variety of clear voices
are heard in collective worship. A voice from the back or several clear
voices calling from different directions can also be very effective.

If there is a sound system in the building don't be afraid to use it.
Create a different atmosphere by using a voice or voices spoken over
the top of quiet music.

A calling voice

The Lord called again, 'Samuel!' . . .

1 Samuel 3.6

God repeatedly calls Samuel until he responds. It is important that we do not over-use or restrict the great wealth of biblical material available for worship. There is, however, value in repetition; repetition aids the memory and allows for extended thinking. Often biblical stories have a number of teaching points, and trying to cover them all in one session leads to confusion or 'information overload'. Create opportunities for pupils to explore stories in greater depth. Each time you return to a story, choose a different focus. Each time pupils encounter the stories, they will bring to them new life experiences.

Isaiah's vision

'Holy, holy holy is the Lord of hosts; the whole earth is full of his glory.'

Isaiah 6.3

Isaiah, the Old Testament prophet, describes an extraordinary vision of God and the heavens. Using the wonder generated by the natural world, architecture or great works of art, we can inspire children to explore their world and to raise 'big' questions about who we are, our origins and our future.

Using video, power point, interactive white boards, overhead transparencies, large posters or pictures, create an extraordinary vision for your children. From a series of images you could take them from immense icebergs to a butterfly in the rain forest, from the ceiling of the Sistine chapel to the Angel of the North.

Angels' voices

And suddenly there was with the angel a multitude of the heavenly host, praising God and saying,

'Glory to God in the highest heaven . . .'

Luke 2.13-14

The Gospel writer, Luke, describes the glorious revelation of the angels to the shepherds; the angels perform a musical spectacular.

Singing is a great way of being bold and having fun. Introduce the children to the rich variety of Christian music, from historic hymns and classical pieces such as Handel's *Messiah* through to African rhythms, Taizé chants and modern action songs. Music gives a sense of the historical, contemporary and multicultural dimensions of Christianity. In the music and lyrics key Christian concepts of love, hope and peace are conveyed and explored.

Music-making also contributes towards building a sense of community and it is, for many, a natural way to worship and to express joy.

Christianity in action

The smallest act has the biggest impact for those who have nothing. Magnify your concern.

Tearfund

Events in the life of Jesus offer examples of ways to be bold in everyday life. The Gospels record how Jesus spent much of his time with people, caring for them, listening, healing and, by example, sharing and revealing the love of God. He was bold in speaking out against injustice and in touching the untouchable. Church schools are challenged to strive to follow this example. They can do this in many different ways: for example, by building sound relationships that embrace all within the school, by working together with the Church and other organizations in the local community and by supporting the work of local, national and international charities.

Act of Worship 1:
The armour of God

Introduction

It is hoped that through taking part in this act of worship the children themselves will begin to feel 'bold'. They are encouraged to 'put on' the armour of God and feel confident in the knowledge that God is with them, in all situations.

The following ideas are suitable for use with the whole school and work particularly well as the theme for an end-of-year leavers' service.

Background

Collective worship themes often focus on the stories of the lives of Jesus and of well-known characters of the Old Testament. Books such as the Acts of the Apostles, the writings of St Paul, Psalms and Proverbs also provide a rich source of themes that can be explored in collective worship. Part of fulfilling the challenge to 'be bold' is to introduce children to many different aspects of the Bible, not just the 'popular' stories.

This act of worship is based on the writing of St Paul in his Letter to the Ephesians (Ephesians 6.10-18). In his letter, Paul challenges the Ephesians to be strong and stand firm, equipped with the whole armour of God. It is often said that education is about preparing children for life. This act of worship emphasizes this concept.

Preparation

This act of worship does need careful preparation but the results make it all worthwhile. Arrange the seating so that there is a wide aisle down the centre.

You will need:

- three or four items of clothing that have a specific purpose: for example, a raincoat, a swimming costume, a pair of football boots, a wedding hat;

- the following signs on pieces of A4 card: belt of truth, breastplate of righteousness, shoes ready with the Gospel of Peace, shield of faith, helmet of salvation, sword of the Spirit;

- a team of volunteers: one child who will tackle the journey of life, with a rucksack containing a map, a bottle of water, a chocolate bar, sun cream and a first aid kit, and a further eight children who will be obstacles in the way.

The eight children need to be in two lines of four facing each other with a two-metre gap between each pair (see diagram). The pathway they now have made down the centre is the journey of life. Each pair need to then use their bodies to make an obstacle across the path, e.g. by swinging arms

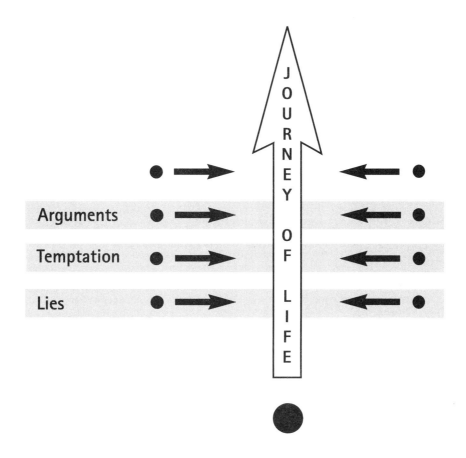

across, doing star jumps, striding backwards and forwards. Three of the pairs have words they must say while making their obstacle movements (see diagram).

Suggested approach

Begin by lighting a candle and using a sentence of welcome. For example:

Leader   The Lord is here.

Response   **His Spirit is with us.**

Explain that you have brought with you a selection of clothes that each have a specific purpose. The clothes have a job to do. Show each item of clothing and ask the children to name it and then tell you when and why you would wear it. If you were wearing X what would you be prepared for? For example, if you were wearing a raincoat you would be ready for rain.

In the New Testament section of the Bible there are many letters written by St Paul. In his letter to the Ephesians he describes clothes that can be worn so that we are ready for life! (You can indicate where, in the Bible, Ephesians is to be found.) Ask your volunteers to go and stand in their positions.

Now have a chat with the child who is going to tackle 'the journey of life' or if you are doing this act of worship as a Leavers' Service you could call it 'the big adventure to high school'. Explain that the pathway, marked out in front, is the journey of life. Do you feel ready to walk along it? Do you feel prepared? Have you got all your equipment? Do you have all you need in your rucksack? (Quickly check through the rucksack.) Announce departure! As the child moves towards the pathway all the obstacles then start moving.

The first pair begin to say their word 'lies' in a loud whisper. The child tries to get through the obstacle but fails. You ask 'Would you like some help?' and they return to stand next to you. Then show them the sign saying 'belt of truth' and put it into the child's rucksack. Say that the child is now equipped to face the first obstacle: as they walk towards it, the obstacle freezes and they walk through. Immediately the next pair begin to say their word 'temptation' and the whole pattern is repeated. This time give the pupil the sign saying 'breastplate of righteousness'. At the next obstacle, 'arguments', give them a sign saying 'shoes ready with the Gospel of Peace'.

Each time, have a chat with the pupil tackling the journey: for example, you could say 'That looked very tricky; I wonder if I have something that will help; do you feel ready now?'

The final obstacle of the journey does not make a noise but is particularly difficult to pass. When the child returns for help, make a comment about the final obstacle being tough. Ask for a name for what it might be. Put the remaining three signs ('shield of faith', 'helmet of salvation' and 'sword of the Spirit') into the rucksack. All can cheer as the journey is successfully completed.

Bring this part to a close by briefly reflecting about the different pieces of 'armour' that helped with the journey. Where did these pieces of armour come from? Which piece of armour is their favourite? Which piece of armour would they need most?

Reflection

Use the overhead transparency on p. 16 as a focus for your reflection time.

St Paul says that the armour of God is available to everybody. We just have to ask God for it and then wear it.

Ask the children to sit very still, close their eyes and imagine they are putting on the armour of God. Slowly name aloud each piece of armour. St Paul finished his instructions with 'Pray . . . at all times.' So let us pray.

> God be with me, God within me,
> God behind me, God before me,
> God beside me, God to win me,
> God to comfort and restore me,
> God beneath me, God above me,
> God in quiet, God in danger,
> God in hearts of all that love me,
> God in words of friend and stranger.

Adaptation of a prayer attributed to St Patrick

Music

The prayer of St Patrick, set to music, can be found on the recording called *The John Rutter Collection*, The Cambridge Singers and the City of London Sinfonia, Universal Classics, 2002.

'Be Bold, Be Strong', No. 14 in *Junior Praise*, Marshall Pickering, 1986, ISBN 0 551 01293 5.

'The Journey of Life', No. 45 in *Come and Praise 1*, BBC Education, 1978, ISBN 0 563 32067 2.

Act of Worship 2:
Lent – A journey towards Easter

Introduction

The aim of this act of worship is to begin exploring the significance of the season of Lent. It would be suitable for use with the whole school or could be adapted for use with other groupings. It would stand alone at any time during Lent but can also work as a series throughout Lent, beginning, for example, on Ash Wednesday.

Following and exploring the Church liturgical calendar provides many opportunities to extend pupils' knowledge of Christian symbolism, practice and values. It can also contribute to a growing understanding of what it means to have faith.

Background

For Christians, Lent is a time of repentance and reflection, 40 days in which to prepare for Easter, the most important festival of the year. Lent is often traditionally associated with giving up something but there is much more to it than that. During Lent, Christians are encouraged to spend more time in prayer and personal reflection. Some follow a special Bible study; abstain from certain foods or drinks; hold fundraising events; and give to charity.

As the themes of Advent lead to Christmas, so Lent leads Christians to Easter with the same sense of anticipation and hope. In Advent the atmosphere of expectancy is encouraged through the opening of doors on an Advent calendar and the lighting of candles. This act of worship tries to create a similar effect through the creation of a 'Lent Line'. The line is constructed in the style of a washing line, where dates, colours, objects and events are added to the line as the weeks move towards Easter.

Preparation

For the basic Lent Line you will need a long piece of string, pegs and coloured cards. Write the following days on the appropriate colour cards in large clear letters: Ash Wednesday (purple), First Sunday in Lent (purple), Second Sunday in Lent (purple), Third Sunday in Lent (purple), Fourth Sunday in Lent, Mothering Sunday (purple), Fifth Sunday of Lent, Passion Sunday (purple), Palm Sunday (red), Monday of Holy Week (red), Tuesday of Holy Week (red), Wednesday of Holy Week (red), Maundy Thursday (red), Good Friday (red), Easter Eve (red) and Easter Sunday (white or gold). You may wish to place thin strips of card in between the Sundays to represent the weekdays. (See diagram on p. 12.)

If you wish to use the Lent Line for an Act of Worship for each week of Lent you will also need:

- a large blank piece of paper

- a giant number 40

- a piece of purple cloth

- a giant pretzel made of paper or card

- a spring flower and a large cross

It is a good idea to secure the string for your Lent Line beforehand and work out the position of the cards on the line to ensure that they all fit!

Suggested approach

Begin by using an opening sentence such as:

Leader   The Lord be with you.

Response   **And also with you.**

Ask if anyone knows what special time of year it is for the Church. What do the pupils already know about Lent? Their responses can be recorded on a flip chart. Use their answers as the basis of your discussion. Some key points and questions you can introduce are that

1. Lent lasts 40 days (make links with the Bible's account of Jesus spending time alone in the desert).

2. It is not Lent every week. I wonder why this might be? Why is Lent a special time for Christians?

3. How do Christians make Lent different from other times in the year?

Lead your questions and discussion to focus upon your 'Lent Line'. Lent is like a journey towards Easter and the Lent Line will be the guide for the journey.

Ask the pupils to help you create the line. (Use the diagram as your guide.)

Spend time exploring the Lent Line: for example, the colours, the number of weeks or the fact that Mothering Sunday is during Lent.

If you are just using the introductory act of worship, go straight to the prayer, given below.

If you are using the Lent Line as the basis for an act of worship throughout Lent, introduce the following objects each week; they give opportunity to explore further the symbolism of Lent.

Week one
A list

Use the list to write down the children's ideas about the different ways in which Christians choose to observe Lent.

Week two
A large number 40

Talk about Jesus spending time in the wilderness for 40 days (Luke 4.1-13). Why did he want to spend time alone? Are there times when we want to be on our own?

Week three
A piece of purple cloth

Purple is the liturgical colour of Lent. Discuss the associations we make between colours and events, emotions, experiences and identity; as an example you might like to consider sports teams. Wonder together about why Lent is purple. (Purple is traditionally associated with royalty; it is a serious, solemn colour.)

Week four
A giant cardboard pretzel

Pretzels are a traditional Lenten food in Germany. Made simply from flour, salt and water (eggs, milk and fats were traditionally not eaten in Lent), the dough is twisted so it resembles two arms crossed in prayer. Pretzels were given as gifts on Ash Wednesday.

Week five
Spring flowers

For Christians, Lent is a time of waiting for the wonder of new life, just as Spring is a time of waiting for new growth, as the natural world bursts into life after a long winter.

Week six
A large cross

Tell the story of Easter Day. Peg the cross onto the line. This is the most important part of the journey of Lent. The cross is the Christian symbol that represents the two sides of Easter: the pain and suffering of Good Friday and the joy and hope of the resurrection of Jesus.

Reflection

Have a dish or tray filled with sand as a reminder of the wilderness where Jesus spent 40 days.

Light a candle for each of the weeks of Lent.

Have some brief moments of silence.

Prayer

Loving God,
as we journey through Lent,
help us to learn more about you,
to care for others and for our world
and to grow in love and hope.
Through Jesus Christ our Lord.
Amen.

Music

'There is singing in the desert', No. 26, or 'From the darkness came light', No. 29, in *Come and Praise 1*, BBC Education, 1978, ISBN 0 563 32067 2.

Act of Worship 3:
St Nina's cross

Introduction

This act of collective worship gives children the opportunity to reflect upon the things in life that are most important to them. It highlights that for some, Jesus is the most significant part of their life. The story of Nina is from the Orthodox Christian tradition.

Background

At the Orthodox Sioni Cathedral in Georgia (part of the Commonwealth of Independent States) there is a unique ancient cross. It is called the cross of St Nina. Around AD 300, Nina, a Christian slave girl, was brought to Georgia to work in the court of the king. Over time she was able to share the Christian story with the king and eventually the whole country adopted the Christian faith. Nina carried with her a cross which was in fact a part of a vine bush. She used this simple twig as a visual aid when telling the Gospel story. St Nina's cross has two distinctive features. The rope symbolizes the way Jesus' followers are to be bound or tied to the service of others and the horizontal cross-piece symbolizes the humility of Jesus and Nina.

Preparation

In order to prepare for this act of worship you will need the design for an overhead transparency of St Nina's cross found on p. 18.

Make a collection of objects which could also be used as starting points for telling stories from the life of Jesus. For example:

- figures from a nativity set for the birth of Jesus;
- a round stone, for the stone that was rolled away from the entrance to Jesus' tomb;
- a loaf of bread, for Jesus' breaking of the bread at the Last Supper;
- a fish, to represent the miraculous catch or the feeding of the five thousand.

Find a twig in the shape of a cross (see the picture on p. 18) for your focus table.

Suggested approach

Use a sentence of introduction such as

Leader	Peace be with you.
Response	**And also with you.**

Project the picture of St Nina's cross (see p. 18) so that everyone can see it clearly.

Ask the children to comment on what they see. What might it be? From what is it made? Is there anything interesting about it? Are there any questions they would like to ask about it? Wonder together about the way it is made.

Tell the story of the cross of St Nina.

> Very little is known about St Nina except this short story. Around AD 300, Nina, a Christian slave girl, was brought to Georgia to work in the court of the king. Over time, she was able to share the Christian story with the king. Eventually the king became a Christian and he proclaimed that his whole kingdom would adopt the Christian faith. In her pocket Nina carried a cross, which was in fact part of a vine bush. (Gesture towards the picture of the cross.) Nina showed great courage and determination. She used this simple twig to help her when she was telling the Gospel story and she told this story because Jesus was the most important thing in her life.

Then show the twig cross and some of the other objects you have collected together. How could they be used to tell one of the stories in Jesus' life? Let the pupils be creative and come up with their own suggestions. Challenge them to make their own collection of objects or pictures for a display in future acts of worship.

Reflection

Light a candle and project the image of St Nina's cross as a focus for attention.

Invite the pupils to think of the people that are most important to them. Ask them to imagine an object that would remind them of that person.

Prayer

Sing the song 'Thank you Lord for this new day' as a prayer. Ask the pupils to suggest ideas for new verses so that they can thank God for the things that are important for them. 'Thank you Lord for this new day' is No. 32 in *Come and Praise 1*, BBC Education, 1978, ISBN 0 563 32067 2.

Be Bold!: OHT for Act of Worship 1

Pretzels are made of
Flour
Salt
Water

The three holes represent the Trinity

They were eaten only during Lent

They were sold in the street to eat with beer or soup

They were first made at the time of the Roman Empire

They were first made by monks. The dough is twisted into the shape of praying arms

In Austria they are hung from palm branches on Palm Sunday

Pretzel Is Traditional Lenten Food

Be Bold!: OHT for Act of Worship 3

Something to think about

Be Bold!

Brainstorm ways in which you would interpret the phrase 'Be Bold!'

> In all circumstances we would recommend that Church schools must be distinctively places where the Christian faith is alive and practised.

The Way Ahead, The Archbishops' Council, 2001, p. 33

- Identify ways in which your school makes a response to this challenge.
- Is it a bold response? Refer back to your brainstorm notes.

> . . . for a Church school, being bold means to dare to be different, to be confident in the faith it represents and to stand out as a holy place; to be a city on a hill.

'Introducing the theme', p. 5

- Identify ways in which your school dares to be different.
- How do you shine like a city on a hill?
- Identify new ways in which your school could respond to this challenge.

Is collective worship in your school 'Bold'?

- Make a list of the positives and the negatives this concept could engender.
- What changes could you make to current practice?
- Is there a need for training or new resources?

Use all these ideas to create a bold vision for the future of collective worship in your school.

Be Creative: OHT Christian symbol – fish

2. Be Creative

Introducing the theme

Imagine you are standing in the corridor of your school. The pupils begin to leave their classrooms and move towards the hall for collective worship. What is the atmosphere in the corridor? Is it one of routine lack of interest or excited expectancy? Only you know the answer to that, but consider which would you prefer: heavy feet or smiles of anticipation?

This chapter offers creativity as a way to generate and encourage the smiles. Creativity is associated with invention, ingenuity and inspiration. Creativity is characterized by originality of thought; it is designed to stimulate imagination and lead to illumination. In collective worship, creativity promotes engagement, enjoyment and enlightenment.

Creativity

'Let me show you something beautiful'
– ritually opening her palm:
a little feather, mostly black,
though touched with grey and brown,
and on its edge the magic yellow
that made me catch my breath.

The yellow brush-stroke made no sense,
nor balance, shape nor form:
Only the artist could foresee
the pattern 'twould build
joining its fellows on the outspread wing
to make an oriental fan,
the glory of the living bird:
Goldfinch – God's finch.

Breandán Ó Madagáin, in Cherish the Earth

Creativity in worship can be revealed in different ways, because what 'catches the breath' of one may not for another. So be creative with stories, technology, images, prayer, silence, poetry, songs, food, artefacts, drama and liturgy. Use current trends in popular culture, such as toys or films, as well as traditional sources. This is not to interpret creativity as novelty or a form of entertainment. Rather, it enables pupils to encounter the Christian faith as a vibrant, living tradition. As well as playing a game, using a puppet or saying a prayer involving actions, there is also value in the simple ritual of lighting a candle and singing a familiar chant.

Collective worship does not have any form of statutory curriculum; therefore the school is free to create its own programme incorporating its needs and interests and capitalizing upon the creative gifts of the staff and pupils. Regularly monitoring and evaluating the programming and planning of collective worship will help to ensure that the senses have been engaged, opportunities to reflect are being given and that the pattern that is being created is full of colour and diversity.

The pupils are being taken on a journey of exploration and discovery; involve them in this process and ask for their opinions about content and the level of enjoyment. The infinite value of spending time being creative is without doubt the pupils' smiles as they walk along the corridor to collective worship; they are expecting to experience 'something beautiful'.

Ways of using the theme

Visual, Auditory, Kinaesthetic (VAK)

People learn best in a variety of ways; we all have different preferred learning and thinking styles. The ways in which we prefer to receive information are identified in three basic types: visual, auditory and kinaesthetic (see, for example, Dryden and Vos, 1994). In curriculum planning, provision is made for pupils to experience different styles of learning and this should also be taken into consideration when planning and leading collective worship. To engage the visual learner, use pictures, objects, word cards, story sacks, video, projected images and guided meditation. Challenge the auditory learner by telling a story using different voices, play a variety of music, use a recorded message and vary the pattern of the worship. Make an impact on the memory of a kinaesthetic learner through action stories and songs, playing games, using prayers involving movement and by dressing up.

Spirituality

Defining what is meant by the term 'spirituality' is notoriously difficult; attempting to do so can lead to a bland consensus definition. Sally Elton-Chalcraft (2002) suggests this can be avoided if spirituality is explored metaphorically as a hologram with four dimensions.

1.   The Inner Dimension – the unique essence of a person and their search for inner meaning

2.   The Social and Moral Dimension – our behaviour and relationships

3.   The Environmental Dimension – being aware of the natural world and the environment around us

4.   The Transcendental Dimension – our response to and deepening understanding of God/the ultimate

Just as the detail of a hologram is revealed only if viewed from several angles, the same could be said of spirituality. This approach offers a framework for creative, collective worship in which pupils can view the 'spirituality hologram' from many angles by exploring the different dimensions.

You don't have to stay inside

Be adventurous and go outdoors! Whether it is the school field or the playground, being out in the fresh air will bring a new atmosphere to worship. Hymns, songs and poems in praise of creation can be more meaningful and inspirational when sung or said in an open-air act of collective worship.

Use stones, twigs, leaves or flowers to stimulate prayers and encourage pupils to use their senses to be alive to what they can see, hear, smell and feel. Ask pupils to collect natural objects from the area around them to create a picture on the ground. Use this as a focus for prayers of thanks for the wonder of creation.

Take advantage of the space to process, to play music, for movement, for drama and for dance.

Are you asking the right questions?

Asking the right questions can make collective worship a vibrant and imaginative experience.

So what is a 'right' question? Questions that are open-ended give opportunity for thought and discussion. They often have many answers that can be wondered about. This approach also acknowledges that there are some questions that have no clear-cut or easy answers; worship leaders do not have to carry the burden of feeling they must always give the 'right' answer.

The style of questioning used in collective worship can really make a difference. By using open questions you will begin to build a bridge between the children's experience and the theme of the story/talk. They will be encouraged to reflect and think about how the theme could make an impact upon their life, beliefs and values.

Once upon a time

A well-told story, fact or fiction, can have a profound impact upon the listener. A story can stimulate memories, laughter and emotion; a story can dance forever in the imagination and become a significant part of a person's spiritual journey. Stories can be told through the use of simple drama or a conversation, a story sack or puppetry, poetry or guided meditation. By using a wide variety of biblical, faith and world stories, pupils are offered the chance to encounter different worlds, visit new people and explore ideas and beliefs about God.

Let's go to the movies

Popular films and television programmes capture the imagination of people of all ages and address issues such as friendship, trust, loyalty, prejudice, jealousy, love, hope and courage; fruitful ground for creative collective worship. Use a film clip, a picture, a toy, or a character like Buzz Lightyear, Shrek or Yoda as a creative introduction to the worship theme.

Games and quizzes

A quick quiz or a game can inject fun and laughter, can engage interest and can illustrate a point. Team games can be used, for example, to emphasize a specific theme or idea, such as working together. Pictures can be created with jigsaw pieces; pupils answer questions and in return receive pieces of a jigsaw. Games like charades could be used to guess who or what a story is about. Be inspired by TV shows: 'Ready, Steady, Cook' a recipe for a good friend; involve parents in a 'Generation Game'; or play a picture round in the style of 'A Question of Sport'. You could create a giant Pictionary on a flip chart or use races to find hidden objects.

The twenty-first century

To ensure that collective worship reflects the contemporary world, the content and presentation need to make a connection with up-to-date developments. On one level this involves looking at themes or stories and relating them to the child's experience. It can also mean exploring the creative use of props such as the latest toy or gadget, using a pop song from the charts, or a phrase from a TV advert. Information technology provides a plethora of tools for creative presentations.

Act of Worship 1
Jesus the teacher

Introduction

This act of worship gives children the opportunity to think about several aspects of the teaching of Jesus. It aims to help pupils see his ministry as a whole, not just as individual events, like pieces of a puzzle. You could use the material for one act of worship, or it could form a series. It would be particularly suitable as a conclusion to a programme of study in RE about the teachings of Jesus. It could be used with children in either key stage, as a whole-school act of worship or in the classroom.

Preparation

You will need a dish of sand and candles to be used for the reflection time.

You will also need to gather together some clues and place them in a covered shoebox or basket. Each object is a clue to remind the pupils of an aspect of Jesus' teaching. Examples are given here but you can be creative and choose others relevant to the pupils' knowledge and experience. The number of objects you choose will depend on the length of time available to you.

A heart –	*Jesus taught about love.*	Jesus gave a new commandment to love one another; love our neighbour and our enemy.
A candle –	*Jesus said, 'I am the light of the world.'*	This phrase tends to be used frequently around Christmas time and children are often very familiar with it. Christians believe Jesus came to shine light and God's love into the 'dark' world. There are many other 'I am' sayings that could be used: for example, 'I am the bread of life' or 'I am the vine.'
A mobile phone –	*Praying is talking and listening to God.*	Jesus emphasized that God listens to everyone at all times, wherever they are.
A sheep –	*Jesus described himself as the Good Shepherd.*	In his teaching Jesus used imagery from everyday life of the time: farming, fishing, flowers and birds. The qualities of a good shepherd are the qualities attributed to Jesus.
A picture of someone in a caring profession –	*Jesus taught people to serve and care for one another.*	Through his words and actions Jesus taught that selfless giving, serving, sharing, helping and caring was the right way to live.
A prayer book –	*The Lord's Prayer.*	Jesus taught the disciples how to pray.
A rock –	*God's word is a solid foundation for life.*	In the story of the two builders, Jesus illustrates that wise people build their lives around the word of God, which is like solid rock.
A 'sorry' letter –	*God forgives.*	Jesus uses the parable of the Lost Son to reveal God's loving forgiveness.

Suggested approach

Place the box/basket of clues onto your worship focus table, to capture the pupils' interest as they enter the hall.

Begin with a sentence of welcome such as:

Leader   Peace be with you.
Response   **And also with you.**

Explain that you are going to be offering the pupils a challenge: to remember some of the things that Jesus taught. Because there are so many, you have brought a box of clues to help. Can the pupils make guesses using the clues as a starting point?

Start with the first object, removing it from the box and displaying it clearly for all to see. Place it on the focus table or attach it to a display board. Ask questions like, 'So, what do you think this might be about?', 'How does this [name of object] remind us of something Jesus taught?'

For each clue, listen to, and explore, the pupils' ideas. Be prepared for a wide range of possibilities, some of which you may not have considered! Encourage the pupils to make connections between their ideas, and links between their experiences and the teachings of Jesus.

Before you move on to the next object, summarize their ideas. For example, if you have been considering the heart symbol, you could say, 'Yes, Jesus did teach that God loves everyone, and that we should try to love each other, even our enemies.'

Reflection

Dim the lights. Project the picture of Jesus teaching a small group of people (which may be found on p. 32). Ask the pupils to be still as they remember the teachings of Jesus.

Use questions to guide the reflection, such as: I wonder what you think was the most important thing Jesus taught? I wonder how people felt as they listened to Jesus? I wonder what they would tell their friends about Jesus as they walked home?

Acknowledge the challenge of Jesus' teachings. Jesus did not say God's ways are easy, but he taught that they are the best ways.

Name each of your 'clues' and the teaching point and, as you do so, light a candle for each one. Watch the light from the candles increase and bring brightness into the room.

Prayer

Jesus' disciples said to him 'Lord, teach us to pray.' He taught them the prayer we now call the Lord's Prayer. This has become the Christian family prayer said by thousands of Christians all around the world every day.

Pray the Lord's Prayer together.

Music

'Lord of the Dance', No. 22 in *Come and Praise 1*, BBC Education, 1978, ISBN 0 563 32067 2.

David Fanshaw's setting of the Latin Mass, *African Sanctus,* fuses African and Western music. Listen to The Lord's Prayer, track 9, Arc Music CD B000093FHF.

Act of Worship 2
Making the right choice

Introduction

This act of collective worship is suitable for whole-school or key-stage worship. It was inspired by these words taken from *Harry Potter and the Chamber of Secrets* by J. K. Rowling (Bloomsbury, 1998, ISBN 0 7475 3848 4):

> It is our choices, Harry, that show what we truly are, far more than our abilities.

Background

We live in a world of 'choice'. Everyone has the 'right' to choose. As consumers we are overwhelmed with choice. Throughout every stage of development pupils are given the opportunity to make choices encouraging them to become independent, decision-making adults. Every day we are faced with a multitude of choices. Knowing what to choose, making choices, considering the effect of those choices and reflecting upon this reveals something of our personality, our values and our worldview. Exploring the concept of choice can enrich pupils' spiritual journeys as they develop knowledge and understanding of themselves and of God.

Preparation

You will need:

- an overhead transparency of the quiz screen (see p. 33)
- four strips of card, numbered one to four, to cover each pair of choices
- a large bar of chocolate
- You will also need to have spoken to staff and made arrangements so that choices two and four can be carried out (see quiz screen, p.33).

Before the pupils enter the room, set up the overhead projector and transparency. Cover the choices with the pieces of card.

There is an element of risk in this approach; you do not know how the pupils will respond to the choices. You may, therefore, wish to consider, before you start, which pupils you are going to invite to be 'contestants'!

The worship leader takes on the role of a 'Game Show' host.

Suggested approach

Begin by making a grand announcement that you are going to play that very well known TV quiz game *Make the Right Choice*. For this, no expense has been spared; you have an amazing electronic quiz screen! Switch on the overhead projector and enthusiastically marvel at the flashing lights and technology. Everything is ready to play the game, so all you need now are four contestants.

Select four pupils to come out to the front. Ask them if they are prepared. Use questions like: Are you ready to make the right choice? Are you good at making the right choice? Do you always make the right choice?

Explain that the rules of the quiz game are simple: all the contestants have to do is *make the right choice!* Begin by introducing contestant number one. Dramatically lift the first piece of card and reveal their choice. (This is the choice about sharing a bar of chocolate.) Ask the child to make a choice between the two options, encouraging them to explain how they made the choice. How did they decide it was the right choice? Involve the rest of the pupils in this discussion; do they think the right choice was made? Why?

Repeat this process with contestant number two. Lift the second piece of card and reveal the choices. This second choice has an effect on the whole school and gives you an opportunity to discuss with the pupils the impact making a choice can have on others. Again explore why the choice was made and use responses as a discussion point.

Continue with contestant number three. Their choice is a moral dilemma. Discuss the options with them and then ask them to make a choice. Have they made the right choice? Was it easy to make this choice? What do the other pupils think? Why?

Finally, with contestant number four, ask if they are ready to make their choice. Follow this with questions like: Are you nervous? Is it easy making choices? Did you agree with the choices made by the others?

Reveal the final choice with a great flourish. This choice asks the child to sacrifice some of his or her own time to help their class teacher. Which choice will they make? Why? Point out that sometimes the choices we make involve sacrificing time, energy or money to help others. You could use examples such as supporting charities, helping parents or siblings, visiting elderly relatives, or spending a holiday carrying out conservation and environmental work.

Once the game is over, give a big cheer for the contestants! Have the bar of chocolate ready to give to the first contestant and remind everyone of the results of choices two and four.

Finish with a short discussion about the concept of choice.

How many choices have the pupils made so far that day? Analyse your day and briefly describe how many choices you have made so far – and it is perhaps only 9.00 a.m. Some choices affect only ourselves; some have a significant impact on the lives of others. Choices can be straightforward and relatively simple: for example, what to wear or which game to play. Other choices can be life changing: for example, choosing friendships, getting married or choosing a career. We also have a choice about the way we behave: choosing between right and wrong, good or bad, to be polite or rude, selfish or selfless. How do we know which is the right choice? All choices have a consequence. We need to consider the outcome when we make the choice.

We may be brilliant at maths, sport, singing or dancing but it is the choices that we make which truly reveal something about the kind of person we are.

Use the quote from Harry Potter (see above).

Throughout our lives there are people who give guidance, and situations and experiences that shape our choices. Christians believe that through prayer and studying the Bible, God gives them guidance and shows them the best way to live their lives.

Readings

To continue and develop this theme further in other acts of worship you could explore the following Bible stories:

- 1 Kings 3 – Solomon chooses wisdom.

- Matthew 4.18-22 and Matthew 9.9 – The Disciples choose to follow Jesus.

- Luke 10.38-42 – Mary chooses to stop and be still.

Reflection

Light a candle and play a piece of quiet music.

Ask the pupils to close their eyes and quietly reflect upon the choices that they have made that day or that week. Have they been the right choices? Who helps them to make the right choice?

Prayer

Dear Father God,
each day I am faced with many choices;
please guide me and help me to know
which are the right choices to make.
Amen.

Songs

'Father I place into your hands', No. 42, in *Junior Praise*, Marshall Pickering, 1986, ISBN 0 551 01293 5.

'Spirit of God', No. 63 in *Come and Praise 1*, BBC Education, 1978, ISBN 0 563 32067 2.

Act of Worship 3
A text message from God

Introduction

This act of worship challenges pupils to think about taking care of the world and the environment in which they live. While suitable for a whole-school act of worship, the material could be used to develop an in-depth discussion of environmental issues appropriate for a group of upper Key Stage 2 pupils.

Background

The focus of this act of worship is placed on the environmental. People of all faiths and of none are concerned about environmental issues. Global warming, pollution, deforestation and the endangering of animal species all pose a threat to the future of our planet, eroding the inheritance of future generations.

People of faith believe that God created the world and entrusted it to our care. This care could extend from using recycling bins to planting new trees. The intention of bringing these issues to the pupils' attention is to help them make their own informed decisions as to what response they wish to make to the challenge of the future of the planet.

Preparation

For this act of worship, you will need:

- an overhead transparency of the mobile phone on p. 34. The screen on the phone has been left blank so that you can write in the text message:

    Please take care of the world. Love from God.

    (You can use it again on other occasions with different messages, if you want to follow a series of collective worships on this theme.)
- a mobile phone
- images of the natural world for display: for example, photographic slides, overhead transparencies, downloaded images or pictures in books or posters
- music to play as pupils enter and leave (refer to the list below)

Suggested approach

Play music as the pupils enter. They should be able to see the images of the natural world, either displayed or projected, as they gather.

Tell the pupils about your astonishment when earlier that morning your mobile phone (remove the phone from your pocket) received a text message from . . . well, they will never guess who it is from . . . such an incredibly important . . . no, they would never guess. Encourage the pupils to give you a few suggestions: perhaps the Queen, maybe a famous sports person, possibly a politician or a film star. Then explain that, no, it was from someone even more extraordinary than that, and that you will now show them. Use the overhead transparency and explain that you have copied the message from your phone so that everyone can see. Look amazed, then say with surprise that it is a message from God! Read the message clearly and pause for a moment.

You now need gently to dissolve this illusion and acknowledge you were having some fun, but the purpose was to try and help everyone think about a serious question. There are many messages from God in the religious scriptures, and in creation stories passed on from one generation to another. Pose questions about it like, 'I wonder what God's message is saying to us?'

Discuss with the pupils the ways in which people respond to creation, both positively and negatively. Make reference to the images of the natural world you have displayed. Explore ways in which we all have responsibilities for the environment. Can the pupils suggest ways they could be doing this?

Reflection

People from different religions and cultures teach that we should respect our environment and care for the planet. Use one or more of these readings as a focus for reflection. (If you choose to do a series of Acts of Worship on this theme, you could use a different reading each time.) Use the images of the natural world, either displayed or projected, during the reading.

> For in him all things in heaven and on earth were created, things visible and invisible . . .
> all things have been created through him and for him.
>
> *Colossians 1.16*

> A wise rabbi was walking along a road when he saw a man planting a tree. The rabbi asked him, 'How many years will it take for this tree to bear fruit?' The man answered that it would take seventy years. The rabbi asked, 'Are you so fit and strong that you expect to live that long and eat its fruit?' The man answered, 'I found a fruitful world because my ancestors planted for me. So I will do the same for my children.'
>
> *Jewish Rabbinic Tale*

> Allah did not want men to stop at looking after animals.
> Plants and trees needed care and respect, too.
>
> 'Even looking after plants and trees is an act of virtue,' said the Prophet.
>
> 'For a Muslim,' he said, 'it is an act of charity to plant a tree or till a land where birds or men or animals come and eat of its fruits.'
>
> *M. S. Kayani,* Love All Creatures, *The Islamic Foundation,1985*

Enjoy the earth gently
Enjoy the earth gently
For if the earth is spoiled
It cannot be repaired
Enjoy the earth gently.

Yoruba poem, West Africa

We are the generation with the awareness of a great danger. We are the ones with the responsibility and the ability to take steps of concrete action before it is too late.

The Dalai Lama

The poem 'Who made all the mess?' by Steve Turner, in *Poems by Steve Turner* selected by Rebecca Winter, Lion, 2002, ISBN 0 7459 4802 2, is also an excellent stimulus for reflection and discussion.

Prayer

Loving God,
we thank you for our beautiful world.
teach us to love our world,
and to take care of it for future generations.
Amen.

Suggestions for music

'What a wonderful world' by Louis Armstrong.

'The Memory of Trees', Enya, Warner Music UK Ltd, 1995.

'All things bright and beautiful' or 'For the beauty of the earth', *The John Rutter Collection*, The Cambridge Singers and the City of London Sinfonia, Universal Classics, 2002.

Songs

'When your Father made the world', No. 73 in *Come and Praise 2*, BBC Education, 1988, ISBN 0 563 34247 1.

'Think of a world without any flowers', No. 17 in *Come and Praise 1*, BBC Education, 1978, ISBN 0 563 32067 2.

Be Creative: OHT for Act of Worship 1

Make the Right Choice – Quiz screen – something like this . . .

MAKE THE RIGHT CHOICE

1	Eat a large bar of chocolate all by yourself.	**OR**	Share a large bar of chocolate with your class.
2	Ten minutes extra playtime with one of your friends.	**OR**	The whole school can have ten minutes extra playtime.
3	Imagine that someone in your class has been taking pencils from the teacher's desk. Nobody knows who it is. At playtime you see someone taking another pencil. What do you do? You talk to your teacher.	**OR**	You say nothing.
4	Spend playtime today helping your class teacher.	**OR**	Spend playtime today and tomorrow helping your class teacher.

Be Creative: OHT for Act of Worship 2

Be Creative: OHT for Act of Worship 3

Something to think about

Be Creative

Imagine you are standing in the corridor of your school. The pupils begin to leave their classrooms and move towards the hall for collective worship. What is the atmosphere in the corridor? Is it one of routine disinterest or excited expectancy?

- Discuss this scenario in groups and then feedback. Through this discussion begin to build a picture of worship in your school, the impact it has on the pupils and their attitude towards it.

- Consider the content, presentation and style of collective worship in your school. How creative are you?

- Does creativity come in short bursts for special occasions or is it a consistent thread running through the whole year? What inspires creativity? What constrains creativity?

- Together look at the paragraphs on pp. 22 and 23 ('Ways of using the theme', above). Consider each paragraph in turn. How could these ideas be incorporated into your current collective worship programme? What changes or additions could you make?

- Take time to discuss and share the creative gifts and talents of the staff. How can these gifts be used to their full potential in worship?

The infinite value of spending time being creative is without doubt the pupils' smiles as they walk along the corridor to collective worship; they are expecting to experience 'something beautiful'. (See Breandán Ó Madagáin's poem on p. 21.)

- How do you interpret the phrase 'something beautiful'? Put together an action plan to implement your vision of 'something beautiful' in collective worship in your school.

Be Creative: OHT for training

Be Still: OHT Christian symbol – dove

3. Be Still

Introducing the theme

Being still is contrary to the daily expectations of life in an increasingly busy school, but attaining stillness and calm can be an important common element in the practice of worship for adults as well as children. This is the case within many faiths as well as Christianity. There are a number of references in the New Testament to Jesus himself wanting to be alone or with a few friends for times of stillness and prayer.

After his baptism, Jesus spent time alone in the wilderness (Matthew 4.1; Mark 1.12-13; Luke 4.1-13).

In Matthew 6.6, Jesus says, 'whenever you pray, go into your room and shut the door and pray to your Father who is in secret'.

In Matthew 17.1, in the event described as Jesus' transfiguration, he again seeks a quiet place: 'Jesus took with him Peter and James and his brother John and led them up a high mountain, by themselves.'

Within the Jewish tradition it is customary to go into a garden for quiet thinking time after the Seder meal at Passover. Jesus went into the Garden of Gethsemane after the Last Supper (Matthew 26.36).

The aim of stillness in the religious traditions is to make an internal space. It is the use of the space that makes it prayerful. This can be achieved by concentration on an object, sound or by holding something. In that inner stillness, meditation and contemplation can take place. In the school situation, collective worship can help children to develop the concentration and reflective skills that are needed to create that inner space. If it is possible for the pupils to hold something in their hands it helps form a link between body and mind connecting the real world with the world inside them. It can be a starting point for the imagination to create internal space. Celtic prayers and songs can be very helpful in making this link.

When one is still and focused, during any event, a greater richness is gained from the experience through the heightened awareness of the senses. Outward stillness can lead to an inward stillness that children and adults need in this frantic stressful culture. Stillness makes silence a possibility. When the pupils are able to be still, short periods of silence can be achieved and these in turn may lead to longer periods. For some people silence is difficult and alien; the space might bring negative thoughts to mind. Some direction of thought should be given to help make it a positive experience.

When inner stillness is achieved it can be a refreshment for that day. This helps both pupils and staff to cope with anxiety or stress and to gain the ability to find inner peace. It can lead to an appreciation of silence as a means of communication and an understanding of how some of the deepest spiritual insights are accessed through stillness and silence.

To be physically still pupils need to be comfortable and have sufficient sitting space so that they are not touching anyone and being distracted. They should feel secure physically and have stillness and calm demonstrated by the adults present. The environment should be as beautiful as possible.

Ways of using the theme

Creating the right atmosphere

Achieving an atmosphere of calm is more likely if all the preparation for the act of worship is completed before the pupils make their entrance. If some pupils are arranging the equipment and focus for the worship make sure that they sit quietly and calmly when all is ready. Strive for quietness before the pupils and staff enter the place of worship, so there is silence on entry. A calm leader who is sitting, rather than standing, shouting, pointing or walking the rows, helps create a calmer atmosphere. A stool or low chair may be used. A wicker-type chair next to a low table can give a relaxed feel to the occasion.

Sacred space

The space used for worship might need attention and even transformation. Look carefully at the space to be used, including the curtains, furniture and displays. Sit where the pupils sit and get a feel for the space and decide whether the furnishings are conducive to creating a sacred space. In transforming the area think of colour, light and darkness, the images and the smells and sounds. Distracting sounds from heating systems and kitchens need to be resolved. If lighting is not sufficiently atmospheric a portable spotlight can be used to great effect.

Think about the surroundings

Banners, posters, textiles, pupils' work, and artefacts can quickly transform an unattractive room into one worthy of worship. They can be made free-standing and placed in front of unattractive objects or attached to things such as the back of a piano to make it beautiful rather than ugly. Fabrics, like lighting, can soften a room or create an atmosphere. Fabrics in the colours of the Church year can be very affective. A focus that is easily seen and colourful also helps create calm; pupils have something to look at and be engaged by. An acetate projected by an overhead projector immediately engages the pupils by its size. Images that include animals or people work well. Pupils' artwork might also be used; or shapes that create a shadow on the screen.

'Please join us for worship'

The presence of adults makes a difference to the occasion. All teaching and non-teaching staff should be present; it gives a sense of unity and the chance for adults to learn from the pupils and pupils to learn from adults. On a practical note, it enables the leader to lead rather than operate crowd control. Stillness is a luxury to many people and it could be a real gift to the staff and pupils to have 15 minutes calm in the day. Occasionally visitors to the school might be invited to join the pupils for worship. They might be from the community or from religious organizations. The invitations might extend to the lollypop person, the caretaker, secretary, governors or friends of the school. A notice might be put at the door, saying, 'Please join us for worship'.

Creating a focus

A focus for worship may be quickly created by covering a table or any piece of equipment with an interesting fabric. Artefacts appropriate to the theme of the worship or to the time of Church year, such as Christmas, Easter or a particular saint's day, might be placed on the fabric. The focus might be added to over a period of time as the theme develops. For example, during Advent a large star could be placed at the back of the hall and gradually be moved forward, so that it is over a nativity scene for the final worship at the end of term.

Symbols of the story

A large variety of objects can be used as a focus. This might be a sturdy candlestick and candle. Thought needs to be given to the most appropriate time for it to be lit and snuffed out. Other suggestions for foci include a display board especially for worship, that is added to daily to generate interest; a water feature; flowers; potted trees or prayer trees; a globe or map of the world; a famous painting; a prayer or thought board; or an attractive box or bag that objects will be taken from during the worship. Symbols of the story might be strategically placed on or around the worship table and then be used in the storytelling or in a tableau.

The focus could also be a pleasant smell pervading the space using incense, an oil burner or a perfumed candle. Use sound as a focus, especially interesting or unusual sounds that need to be listened to for a long time: a rain stick, a drum or Buddhist singing bowl. If music is played as pupils enter for their worship it should be faded out rather than stopped abruptly, to maintain the calm effect.

Using the natural world

In good weather windows may be opened to listen to the bird song, wind in the trees or other sounds. Small numbers of children might go on a listening walk for their worship or sit in a garden area of the school grounds. Keep baskets of objects so each child may have something of their own to hold during worship. It might be a pebble, conker, shell, acorn or piece of material. On other occasions it might be a flower, leaf or imaginary object that is held in silence as a story is told, a poem read, a prayer said or during a time of silent reflection.

Signing

Signing can be a powerful contribution to worship. It might be used in opening or closing the worship. For example, pointing to the sky, pointing to the ground and pointing to each other to say 'God is here with us'. The Lord's Prayer or a school prayer may be signed. Learning the prayers through signing is a valuable way to understand the meaning of the prayers. Hand movements and signs can be used in storytelling too. Try using Indian dance hand movements; develop different non-verbal ways of communication.

Act of Worship 1
A special place to go

Introduction to the theme and its purpose

A significant element of people's spiritual development is access to creative and imaginative activities. It is important for pupils to be given tasks and experiences that tap into and extend their creative and imaginative insights. This particular act of worship gives opportunities for the participants to use their imaginations to explore special places where one can find comfort, help and wonderment.

Preparation

You will need:

- either a print of an Impressionist picture, for example Monet's 'Water-garden at Giverny', or a poem about a beautiful place, for example William Wordsworth's 'Daffodils' or John Masefield's 'Sea Fever' (see *One Hundred Great Poems*, selected by Victoria Parker, Miles Kelly Publishers Ltd, 2000, ISBN 1 90294 754 1).

- calm, soft, lyrical music: for example, Debussy's 'La fille au cheveux de lin' ('The girl with the flaxen hair').

Suggested approach

Have calm music playing as the pupils enter quietly.

Light a candle to signify the start of worship.

Either begin by using an image:

Listen to Debussy's 'La fille au cheveux de lin', which is a lyrical and gentle melody played on the piano. As the music is playing, talk quietly about the images it creates in your mind: build a lyrical verbal picture in words of where the music takes you and the children; explore why it creates these images and not others, e.g. soldiers marching, nightmares, fear; share and qualify your opinion of the music; and hear the opinions of the children. Encourage them to say why they have these thoughts.

Or begin by using a poem:

Read the poem slowly and with real expression and feeling; it has real power. Explore the poem's meaning with the pupils: what the writer loved about the place; what phrases and words were used by the writer to show this.

Tell the children that you are now going to take them somewhere else that is very special, very beautiful and very peaceful. Suggest they either close their eyes or stare at the candle to help them imagine this place.

Guide their imagination using short simple phrases:

Imagine a special place to go to be quiet, to be alone, to think or to pray. It might be a seat at the bottom of the garden, enclosed by plants, trees, or fields. (It is important to be lyrical and descriptive.)

Pose questions like: What do you do in your special place? When can you go there? How do you feel there? Are there other people in your special place? Leave gaps of silence between the questions.

Gently bring the children's thoughts back to the present. Some children may wish to share details of their own special place.

Prayer

> Thank you God
> for special places,
> for quietness and peace
> and for times to be alone.
> Amen.

Song
'Peace, perfect peace', No. 53 in *Come and Praise 1*, BBC Education, 1978, ISBN 0 563 32067 2.

Suggestions for music
Debussy, 'La fille aux cheveux de lin'.

Other music:

Mozart, Clarinet Concerto, second movement.

Fauré, 'Pie Jesu' from *Requiem*.

Rachmaninov, *Rhapsody on a theme of Paganini*.

Dvorak, Symphony No. 9, *From the New World*, second movement, Largo.

Myers, 'Cavatina'.

Debussy, 'Clair de lune'.

Act of Worship 2
Listening to God

Background

In this act of worship the story of Samuel is used to illustrate the concept of listening to God. It would also fit other worship themes: for example, 'People of Faith', 'Stories from the Bible' or 'Commitment'. Whatever the theme, endeavour to engender a sense of calm and stillness when telling the story through the vocabulary you use and the tone of your voice.

Preparation

Create a calm atmosphere with appropriate gentle music and subdued lighting.

You will need a large box, lit by a spotlight or candle. This will be the focus for the story and the prayer. The worship leader should be sitting to one side, in the role of storyteller.

The Bible reference for this story is 1 Samuel 3.1-21. Read the story for yourself and then read it as it has been retold in this Act of Worship. You may wish to adapt it, to reflect your own storytelling style.

Suggested approach

Simple stilling exercises help children to be relaxed and alert. Suggest that they tense their fists and shoulders and then relax them. Then take deep breaths while the leader counts to four, in and out, two or three times. Then prepare for the story; closing eyes is one way to aid concentration. One of the traditions of storytelling is to signal the beginning of a story, or a quiet, reflective time, with a distinctive sound: for example a gentle gong, a Buddhist singing bowl or rainstick. Use these techniques on a regular basis to focus attention and to develop the skill of listening attentively. You will find the silence will be profound.

Set the scene . . .

Worship leader (see note above): 'We are in Israel, approximately 3,000 years ago. A young woman called Hannah had prayed for many years and asked God for a child. When she eventually had a son she dedicated him to God, and he was brought up by Eli, an old priest in the temple. Eli was almost blind. He slept in one room and Samuel slept in the sanctuary, where the sacred Covenant Box was kept. This was the box that contained the teachings of Moses, the Ten Commandments.'

Present the story . . .

> Samuel lay drifting between sleep and waking in the last shadow of night before dawn. The lamp still burned in the sanctuary where he slept, causing the shadows to dance across the great Covenant Box. Samuel could hear the heavy rumble of Eli's breathing next door, and his eyes closed once again, consciousness flowing away. 'Samuel, Samuel,' a voice was calling, repeating his name, like the rush of the tide on shingle. Samuel sat up, startled.

He ran to Eli and said, 'Yes, sir, you called me – here I am.' Eli said that he did not call – and that Samuel should go back to bed. The voice called again and Samuel went once more to Eli's bedside. Once again Eli said that it was not him calling. Samuel returned to his bed. The voice called Samuel a third time and once more he went to see Eli. This time Eli, in his wisdom, realized that it was in fact God calling Samuel. So he told the boy that the next time he heard the voice call his name he must answer, 'Speak, Lord, your servant is listening!'

Samuel did just as Eli said. When he heard the voice calling his name he said, 'Speak, Lord, your servant is listening!' God told him about what he intended to do over the coming years. Samuel passed the messages on to Eli and, many years later, all that he had been told came to be. Everyone knew that Samuel was a true prophet – someone who listened and heard God's word.

Gently return the children's attention to the present.

Wonder together about the story using some of the following questions:

- What is interesting, puzzling or surprising about the story?

- What questions does the story raise?

- What does the story make you think about?

- How does the story make you feel?

The worship leader or another member of staff could share their thoughts on a time when they have been in a 'holy' or special place and they have felt close to God.

This could be followed in subsequent days by a visitor to the school sharing their experience.

Song

'Kum ba yah', No. 68 in *Come and Praise 1*, BBC Education, 1978, ISBN 0 563 32067 2.

Prayer

Use the storytelling signal (see 'Suggested approach') and invite the pupils to listen to the sound. Draw their attention to the box you have used for the focus of the story.

Ask the questions 'Imagine this box contains something very important to you. What might it be?' 'Why is it important to you?' Use the OHT on p. 47 as a focus for your thoughts.

Play some soft music as the pupils leave in silence.

During the week the box can be used as a focus for special thoughts. Ask pupils and teachers to write down their thoughts and some of these might be shared. (Be sensitive to those who would prefer their thoughts not to be shared.)

Music suggestions

Use the same music for entrance and exit.

Dvorak, Symphony No. 9, *From the New World*, second movement.

Massenet, 'Meditation' from *Thais*.

Mozart, Clarinet Concerto, second movement.

Act of Worship 3
In times of sadness

Introduction to the theme and its purpose

This act of worship was developed by Ann Parry Jones, from Ruskington Chestnut Street Church of England Primary School (Diocese of Lincoln), in response to a devastating flood in Mozambique. A similar pattern of worship could be used in the event of a death or other tragic circumstance, whether close to home or in a distant part of the world. It gives the opportunity to voice concerns and share memories.

Background

Sadly each year brings major concerns. We all react differently and need different outlets for our anxieties and our grief. For Christians, the ritual of prayer, stillness and quiet reflection creates a dignified space in which to remember those concerned in each difficult or tragic situation.

Preparation

A series of images needs to be prepared that are relevant to the current issue. Overhead transparencies or a Powerpoint presentation may be created from photographs or newspaper cuttings (which may be downloaded from the Internet).

Prepare class teachers for the seating arrangement. If possible, groups of children should form wedge shapes, or blocks, around the focal point. There should be several pathways, between the wedges, to the centre and outer edges. Ensure all the children can see the image.

Arrange the room with a low table, as the focal point, in the centre of the space. Place a large number of night lights and one large candle on the table. (Have water or sand on hand for fire safety.)

Prepare participants to contribute thoughts or concerns on the theme of the act of worship.

Suggested approach

- Dim the lights. Make sure that there are no disturbing sounds and play appropriate music as people enter.

- Introduce the theme as the candles are lit.

- Use the image(s) to talk about the situation and the concerns. If it is a memorial, reflect on all the happy, funny or quirky memories of the person. Several people may contribute to this.

- Between thoughts, or groups of thoughts, sing the Taizé chant 'O Lord, hear our prayer'.

- Leaving an image on the screen, ask for the contributions from pupils who have prepared thoughts, poems, prayers and hopes.

- Rather than closing eyes and putting hands together for the prayers, everyone can hold hands for a final reflection.

- Alternatively, the worship leader can invite everyone to cup their hands and imagine the person or people concerned being held in their hearts and minds and/or in God's hands.

Prayer/reflection

End in a time of silence, using the overhead transparency (see p. 48) as a focus.

Music

'Libera', Libera Erato Disques, Warner Music CD 3984 290532.

Song

'O Lord, hear our prayer', from *Music from Taizé* (Vocal Edition), Collins, 1982.

CD *Songs of Taizé*, boxed set £16.99, number 5019282221022.

NAMASTE
peace be
with you
Shalom salaam

What is important for you?

Be Still: OHT for Act of Worship 3

Something to think about

Be Still

■ For Christians, worship incorporates reflective meditative experiences. Identify ways in which quiet and silence could enhance school worship.

■ Consider the number of occasions in the school day when there is absolute quiet or silence. Suggest times in the day, other than in collective worship, when silence might be achieved. How might the time be used and for what purpose?

■ How could the worship area in school be developed to enable a calm and quiet atmosphere? What artefacts might aid this process? What changes, in timing, location, routine, could be made?

■ What training of staff and pupils needs to be done in order to create stillness during the worship?

■ Consider ways of being reflective other than in silence.

■ How can stillness be used to promote:

   (a) the spiritual development of pupils;

   (b) the spiritual life of the adults attending worship;

   (c) the ethos of the school?

Be Thoughtful: OHT Christian symbol – Gospel emblems

4. Be Thoughtful

Introducing the theme

Personal experience has more impact on an individual's search for self-knowledge than experience handed on from another. The only way to understand something is to engage with it. To develop thoughtfulness, appropriate questions need to be asked and answers heard and considered. The majority of those leading of acts of worship use the question and answer technique to engage pupils' attention, but questions need to be probing and challenging in order to develop deeper thoughtfulness in all pupils.

At the heart of religious experience is what it means to be human. Worship is a place where the big questions concerning goodness, suffering, hope, love, commitment and the ultimate should be asked. Such concepts are a reality for young people as well as for adults; part of our shared human experience. Pupils will recognize the pain of illness or unfair treatment. Some may well have experienced disaster, death or rejection. They will be able to recall their responses. In worship, a safe environment should be created for reflection and consideration of different views on these issues, in order to help make sense of situations that can seem to be beyond our understanding.

People of faith believe that guidance on how they should lead their lives comes from the teachings of their religious leaders and from their holy books; they believe that this is the path to fulfilment. Moral values come from what believers regard as religious truth. For Christians this is ultimately that God is the creator and therefore knows what is best for each individual.

In exploring beliefs and values for living taught by Christianity and other worldviews, pupils are given opportunities to reflect on a range of ideals and convictions. These are the tools by which people make decisions about what really matters in life. In turn pupils should be given the chance to reflect on their own values and those of society today. This gives an opportunity to develop thinking skills and to learn to empathize with others. By offering thought-provoking acts of worship, pupils and teachers can reflect together with a clear sense of purpose.

Ways of using the theme

Question and answer

The question and answer technique is the most widely used method of including pupils in an act of worship. It must always be sensitively done so that the pupil is affirmed and never humiliated. This is usually done well by teachers but perhaps visitors need reminding, so that pupils do not suffer a loss of confidence. Opportunities should also be given for the pupils to ask questions of the leader. This might become a ritual in one particular act of worship each week or each month.

Thought boards

A thought board, similar to a prayer board, can have a place in the worship area, in the entrance to the school, in a corridor or classroom. One design is to have a pattern of crossed ribbons over a board, enabling the pupils to attach their prayers easily. Pieces of card should be close by, with a pen. Use different shaped cards like thought clouds, seed pods or stars to attract fresh interest. Thoughts about national and international issues of concern can be featured as well as personal situations. Some may be expressed as prayers, or poems. Use them in worship or as a focus for quiet reflective times.

I wonder . . . ?

Inclusive questions that are open to all are a good way to encourage pupil involvement. They also give opportunities for imaginative answers, and imagination is an important ingredient in spiritual development. To experience mystery we have to conceive things which go beyond the known and the ordinary, and this requires a rich imagination. Stimulate creative and imaginative thinking by opening a story using a large piece of material thrown over a table or in the centre of a circle. Ask the question 'I wonder what this might be?' As the pupils respond with many answers use responses like 'It might be . . .', and then eventually say, 'but today it is a . . .' (whatever forms the setting for the story). Other objects can be placed on the cloth and again the 'I wonder' questions can be asked to encourage pupils' involvement in the story: 'I wonder what the writer of the story wanted to tell us?' and 'I wonder what the story is saying to us?' or after looking at a painting, 'I wonder what the artist wanted to say?'

Making connections

Descriptive questions can be equally inclusive because the pupils have access to some experience which will give them a means of answering. Use any artefact, or a piece of art work, and ask the pupils to describe what they see. Inevitably different pupils will notice different things. Encourage the pupils to make connections and the discussion can be guided towards the particular theme that is being explored. Equally the pupils can be asked to describe what they hear when they listen to a particular piece of music or what they smell or touch. This can be a way of extending the sensory experience and vocabulary.

Knowing when to ask the question

Professional judgement is required to decide whether or not it is the correct moment to gather responses to reflective questions during the act of worship. This is particularly relevant in relation to questions about feelings. Sometimes, it is sufficient to pose a question and leave it with the pupils to ponder. If appropriate, teachers can provide opportunities for pupils to share their reflections on worship themes at other times in the day.

Digging deeper

Going beyond the descriptive is a way to develop deeper insights. Using a piece of art, a story, or a poem, ask questions of it, for example:

- What is interesting, puzzling or surprising about it?

- What judgements are made in the picture/story/poem?

- How do you know?

- What questions does it raise?

- What does the mood of the picture/story/poem add to or detract from the theme?

- What does it make you think about?

- Do these feelings or thoughts clash or do they work together?

It may be possible to compare the painting/story/poem with the text on which it is based.

Challenging times

It is appropriate to have spontaneous acts of worship when there are major national or international events or there is a school crisis. The values that the school holds dear may well be ones that at these times are reinforced or challenged. Each occasion will require a decision as to the extent of discussion and questioning that is appropriate for the particular context. It is important, however, that pupils have a 'safe' place to raise difficult or troubling questions and that they know their questions will be taken seriously.

Plant a tree in the school grounds as 'The Peace Tree' or 'Tree of Hope'. If this is not possible, build a peace pole: www.peacepoles.com gives ideas for making your own. Use the area as the focus for particular days and annual events such as Holocaust Day on 27 January or Remembrance Day on 11 November; during One World Week or the Week of Prayer for World Peace; or on the anniversary of the death of someone in the community.

Challenging questions

Use probing questions that extend thinking and go beyond the superficial. Examples of these are: Please explain what you said or explain further: Why might that be? Can you think of a reason? Suggest a reason for . . . or suggest other reasons for . . . or put the opposite point of view. Can you point to some evidence? What tells you that this is correct? Why do you say that? Do you believe that? Why do some people believe that? The questions must be asked in a gentle, encouraging way, as the questions themselves are challenging.

Act of Worship 1
Transfiguration

Introduction to the theme and its purpose

This act of worship might well be linked with religious education or worship themes on 'special times', 'ourselves', 'seeing the special nature of others' or 'transformation'. The purpose is to give the pupils insight into the event Christians call the Transfiguration and to offer reflections on the importance of appreciating and nurturing our inner selves.

Background

Moses and Elijah were the two great prophets of the Old Testament. Moses represents the law. He received the law from God in the wilderness; a covenant or agreement between God and his people. Elijah represents the prophets who foretold the coming of the Messiah. The event Christians call the Transfiguration is described in three of the Gospels (Luke 9.28-36; Matthew 17.1-8; Mark 9.2-8). (Use Matthew's Gospel if you wish to read it dramatically.) Jesus talks with Moses and Elijah; the Gospel writers are describing Jesus as the fulfilment of the law and the word of the prophets.

The traditional Jewish teaching was that Elijah must appear again before the coming of the Messiah (based on Malachi 4.5-6). Jesus' disciples, on this occasion, reasoned that if Jesus was the Messiah, as the transfiguration suggested, why had Elijah not reappeared? The story illustrates that just as John the Baptist was not recognized by his contemporaries, so Jesus would not be. The significance is that in a fleeting moment, those close friends of Jesus, Peter, James and John, suddenly see a different side to him. They become aware of his very special nature; they literally see him in a new light.

In life, we occasionally see others as they really are; we see something of what has previously been hidden. We use the expression, 'I have seen him/her in a new light.'

Preparation

Prepare the cube shape (see p. 60) for projection.

Pupils should have been prepared to read the story of the Transfiguration (Matthew 17.1-8). To make this a dramatic reading, divide the text between a narrator, Jesus, Peter, James and John.

Suggested approach

- Project the image of the cube shape as the pupils enter.

- Invite the pupils to look at the image and say what they can see.

- Discuss the pupils' responses to the image. Have they observed the movement of one image to another? One moment the outside of the box can change and become the inside of the box.

- Talk about the outer images people project and how these might be different to the way they feel inside. For example, a person may appear to be outgoing, noisy and fun-loving, yet inside they might be sensitive, easily hurt, or reserved.

- Talk about spotting 'another side' of someone you know well. For example, when you have all been on an outing, or residential visit, you may have seen a completely different side to a person as you spotted something of their inner qualities.

- Tell or read the story of the Transfiguration, when the close friends of Jesus saw him in a different way.

Then pose some of the following questions:

- What reasons might Jesus have had for keeping his thoughts about himself, to himself?

- What might have happened just before this incident to cause his friends to recognize this change in him?

- What reasons do we have for keeping our inner selves hidden?

- How do we get to know the person we are inside? How do we help that person to grow?

Making popcorn provides a dramatic visual image of the concept of change and transformation, especially the idea of the inside of something becoming visible on the outside. Try making popcorn as a follow-up activity to this act of worship!

Prayer

Use the image of the cube as the focus (see p. 60).

> Lord, let us always be ready to look at every situation and every person over
> and over again.
> Help us to see what is really important and what is right.
> Help us to understand how special we are and know that this can grow,
> so that we do what is important and what is right.
> We ask this in Jesus' name,
> Amen.

Act of Worship 2
Possibilities . . .

Introduction to the theme and its purpose

The purpose of the act of worship is to reflect the Christian belief that each life is full of possibility and potential. Circumstance and choice can restrict these possibilities but for people of faith, there is always hope; God is present in all choices and decisions and in the living out of the implications.

Background

This act of worship focuses on the story of Joseph (Genesis 37.1-11 and 23-28). The approach could also be used for any one of a number of Bible characters: for example, Ruth, David, Esther, or Paul. Each of these characters became restricted by circumstances but through a faith in God achieved far greater things than would have seemed possible.

Pupils are encouraged to enter the stories and reflect on how they relate to their own experience.

Preparation

A space is required for a group of pupils to move about and to act out the story.

Prepare the pupils for their roles in the story.

The worship leader needs to be familiar with the events in the story. Either tell the story in your own words or use a simple retelling from a children's Bible.

Suggested approach

Introduce the first part of the story of Joseph (Genesis 37). Involve the pupils in acting out the story.

- Joseph, the youngest in his family, was the favourite of his father. His brothers were jealous and hated him (vv. 2-4)

- Joseph's first dream (vv. 5-8)

- Joseph's second dream (vv. 9-11)

- Joseph's brothers take action (vv. 23-28)

At the end of each stage, pause (your actors could use the 'freeze-frame' technique) and engage the pupils in a brief discussion about the characters in the story. Encourage them to think about each of the characters: how might they feel; consider their motivations for action; ask pupils to make links with their own experience.

Finish the storytelling at the point where Joseph arrives in Egypt as a slave. He knows no one; he is missing his family and feels completely alone; he has time to reflect on what has happened to him. His response is to pray to God. In spite of all the things that have happened he always believes that God is with him.

Invite pupils to consider how Joseph feels at this point in the story. What sort of regrets might he have had about the past? About the way he had treated his brothers? About the way he had talked to his family about his dreams?

This story has an interesting twist, because Joseph found he was able to interpret dreams. He was able to help the Egyptian Pharaoh and became a trusted servant and a very important person in Egypt. He was in a position to give a home to all his brothers, who were suffering from a famine in their land. No one could ever have thought or even dreamt that he could have achieved such things, but Joseph believed that God was always with him and so, wherever he was, he would find opportunities to do God's work.

Reflection and Prayer

Light a candle.

Many people who have found themselves alone, or in a strange place, have found comfort by praying to God. Project the picture of a kite flying freely (see p. 61).

Invite the pupils to remember in their thoughts and prayers:

- something that is important for them today;

- something for which they are sorry;

- something for which they are thankful.

Have a time of silence.

End by saying the Lord's Prayer.

Music

Africans who were taken as slaves to America composed 'spirituals'. These are songs that are prayers to God.

Listen to, or sing, spirituals such as 'Swing low, sweet chariot', or 'I'm gonna sing, sing, sing, I'm gonna dance, dance, dance', or 'Oh, when the saints go marching in'.

Act of Worship 3
Taking risks

Introduction to the theme and its purpose

Risk is an essential part of human development and *not* taking risks can be like doing nothing. Risk enables us to fulfil our potential by making us more courageous and adventurous. It also helps us to appreciate those who take risks on our behalf. For Christians, Jesus provides an example of this. He stood alongside the vulnerable, the oppressed, the diseased and those living on the edge of society. He dared to challenge the accepted norms of the time and his radical stance cost him his life. His actions give hope and a new view of life for those who follow his way and his teachings.

Background

This worship links with many PSHE and citizenship themes. Risk is an important ingredient in what it means to be human, but within this context it is about engaging the pupils in order to think and reflect on solidarity with others; standing up and being counted; making choices about the environment and our lifestyles.

A number of Bible stories are suitable to illustrate this theme. The story of the Good Samaritan is used in this act of worship. Other examples would be the journeys of Paul or Jesus' healing miracles.

Anyone who has achieved anything notable has incurred risk. The emphasis is on taking risks for the betterment of others, especially the vulnerable. This includes animals and the environment.

Preparation

Identify volunteers for the 'trust' game.

Prepare pupils for their involvement in the storytelling: for example, as readers, or as actors.

Suggested approach

- Start by playing a trust game. For example, choose eight volunteers to come out to the front. Ask six to sit on the floor in pairs opposite each other, with feet stretched out and touching. Blindfold one of the two that are left. The other is to lead the blindfolded person safely across the length of outstretched legs. When this is completed, ask questions of your volunteers. How did it feel to do this? Who was taking the bigger risk? Was it easy to trust each other? Can you say why?

- Tell the story of the Good Samaritan (Luke 10.25-37). Involve pupils in the telling.

- Take each of the characters in turn and ask questions of them. Try to see the event from their point of view. Are there parts of the story that surprise you?

- Wonder together about the story. For example ask questions such as: I wonder who is taking the bigger risk in this story? I wonder who is gaining most in this story?

- Ask the pupils to think of ways they have taken, or could take, risks. What would be the implications; the possible gains; the possible losses?

Prayer

The words of St Ignatius of Loyola form a well-known traditional prayer (see p. 62). Invite pupils to suggest simple actions (or use signing) to accompany each line of the prayer. Then either say, with actions, or simply mime the prayer all together.

This is a very good way to think through a prayer and it shows another way of praying: with our whole bodies.

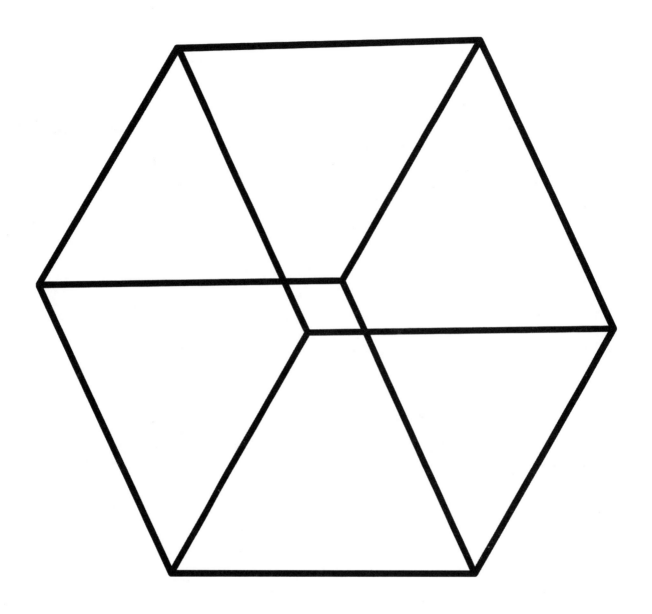

Be Thoughtful: OHT for Act of Worship 1

Be Thoughtful: OHT for Act of Worship 2

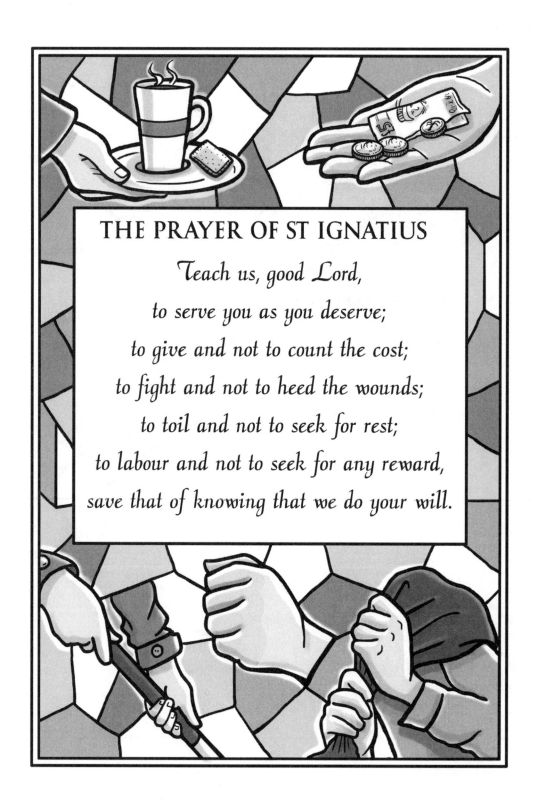

THE PRAYER OF ST IGNATIUS

Teach us, good Lord,

to serve you as you deserve;

to give and not to count the cost;

to fight and not to heed the wounds;

to toil and not to seek for rest;

to labour and not to seek for any reward,

save that of knowing that we do your will.

Something to think about

Be Thoughtful

■ For Christians, worship has a teaching and learning element where the big questions are explored. Identify some of the big issues that might be considered in your school worship programme.

■ How often are challenging questions or issues presented in acts of worship? Reflect on experiences that have been most helpful and thought-provoking.

■ What needs to happen to maximize the opportunity for worship discussions to be followed up in the classroom?

■ Are there any opportunities in the school day for the pupils to consider the big questions? How can open-ended questions facilitate this process?

■ Make a list of questions to extend or deepen the pupils' responses, for example: What might that be? Can you explain that? Can you think of a reason?

■ In what ways are the worship leader's responses to pupils important in this process? Make a list of open-ended responses that teachers might use when dealing with unanswerable or complex questions: for example, 'I have always wondered that myself.'

■ What is the value of questions like 'I wonder . . .'?

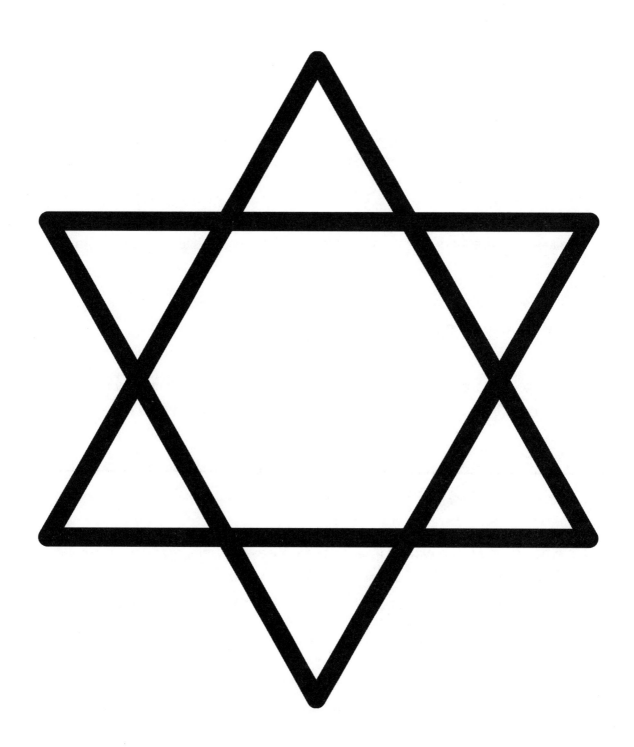

Be Humorous: OHT Christian symbol – star of creation

5. Be Humorous

Introducing the theme

It is OK to laugh in worship. This does not mean collective worship should be a joke-telling session, but it does mean that smiling, laughter and fun can be a component of worship and there are many funny stories in the faith traditions. Apart from the fact that these things make one feel physically better, they help create an ethos that is comfortable for sharing ideas and thoughts.

Laughter can dissipate tension. One of the great strengths of humour in worship is that it enables the leader to open up difficult issues and create an atmosphere in which serious matters can be explored comfortably. As a general rule of thumb, the humour should never be at the expense of anyone other than the leader.

Major issues such as racism, disability, injustice and suffering can be discussed more fruitfully in a secure, relaxed atmosphere. Taboo or sensitive subjects, such as dreams, visions and death, can also be approached in this way.

From the evidence of theologians, who have put the parables and sayings of Jesus into context, he must have been a 'funny, charismatic guy'. His listeners would have been amused by the incongruity of his stories. They would be aware that farmers do not scatter precious seeds far and wide as in the story of the Sower (Luke 8.4-15) or leave their sheep while they look for a lost one, as in the story of the Good Shepherd (Luke 15.1-7).

It was the incongruity and humour that would have engaged his listeners and then led them into thoughtfulness about this particular new way of looking at the world. For the majority of the time, Jesus, in his teaching, was actually suggesting a worldview that contradicted the accepted worldview of his time.

In school we are often doing just this, presenting views that are not in tune with the codes received at home and from the media, and so it is important to find ways of engaging with the pupils as a starting point.

A sense of humour is a wonderful gift that should be celebrated. Worship is a place where gifts and talents are brought before God. Humour has an equal place with music, art, dance and language. When communities or groups laugh together it creates a feeling of closeness and well-being. Genuine laughter is a physical and spiritual tonic, as it creates happiness. Laughter is a good way to start a school day. It helps to put life into perspective and reduce stress. It is one expression of joy, which is a spiritual experience.

It must be remembered that not everyone has the facility to be amusing in a worship situation and if they try and fail it can be counter-productive. Sometimes it is necessary to be cruel to be kind with one's colleagues and to advise them on their best forms of delivering worship. Success is more likely when people relax and are themselves, sharing their own humour rather than mimicking their favourite comedian.

A light-hearted atmosphere can be created in a number of ways.

Ways of using the theme

Body language

Body language can be crucial in creating a light-hearted atmosphere. A relaxed rather than a tense body posture should be adopted; a sitting position rather than a standing position can help the pupils feel more at ease. This is especially so if they are small and sitting in the front row. It is good to consider the view that the pupils have from their particular situation.

Facial expressions are paramount in humour. The gentle face that tells amazing stories or the fierce face that tells of fearsome events or the animated face that takes on the various characters in the story can be equally amusing. When body movements and facial expressions come together to be the monkey, the grumpy grandfather or the enthusiastic disciple Peter, powerful images are created that the listener will more easily remember. For further fun the pupils can be encouraged, through the course of a story or a shared experience, to copy the movements demonstrated by the leader.

The voice

Use of the voice is a way of creating amusement, particularly if the worship leader is able to mimic dialects. If the leader can immerse him or herself in this way, the story becomes more amusing and believable. To be able to take on different voices when telling a story is a wonderful ability and helps the pupils and the storyteller to be more involved in the story. If the storyteller finds this difficult, use some of the pupils or teachers (who have been previously primed) to be the different voices. Some teachers and pupils are born comedians.

Using humour

The choice of content of the worship might in itself be humorous. It can be something that has happened to the leader, or happened in school, or it might be a humorous story from one of the faith traditions. The Hindu stories of Ganesha, and how he got his elephant's head, and the many playful antics of Krishna, like the story of Krishna and the milk maidens, are great sources of fun and amusement. In the Christian tradition, Jesus describes the comical scenario of a camel trying to get through the eye of a needle (Matthew 19.24); his parables would have seemed so outrageous to his listeners that they would have been greatly amused by them. This is the strength of these stories because they beg the question, 'What is the truth of the story?'

Amusing secular stories or poems also have an important place in worship as they can be a means of exploring difficult and sensitive issues. Examples of these include Alan Ahlberg's poem about bullying, 'The Boy without a Name', in *Heard it in the Playground*, Alan Ahlberg, Puffin Books, 1991, ISBN 01403282460, and 'The Fib' by George Layton, in *The Fib and Other Stories*, George Leyton, Macmillan Children's Books, 2001, ISBN 0 330 39795 8.

Language

Amusing language is tool that can be used effectively to engage pupils. Any word that might seem a little naughty, or a word that they would not expect a teacher to use, is amusement, but also helps to put the message across. Repetition of words in stories or songs is another useful device to amuse. It can also be fun to sequentially stop using words and mime them instead, as in the song 'Father Abraham', where the instrument is mimed rather than named. As it speeds up it becomes even more fun.

Artefacts and props

Use of props can be a lively way to bring a story or situation to life. Choose artefacts and props that help to focus attention; a box of hats, head-dresses or scarves can be a valuable aid. Funny glasses and a wide variety of headgear are freely available. Quite easily, a gardener, fairy or professor can be outfitted with a cap and scarf, wand and glittery headgear or glasses and a wig.

Puppets and masks

Puppets and masks engage pupils of all ages. Puppets are a wonderful device for creating rapport with people. They have the advantage of being able to say and do silly things which a teacher or headteacher normally could not do. They can ask pointed and deep questions while seeming to be amusing or innocent.

Pupils can make their own masks, or custom-made ones can be collected. They too have the advantage of the wearer being able to say or do outrageous things that can promote amusement while being a stimulus for serious discussion.

Clowning around

'Clowning' is a concept that has always been used as a way of stimulating deep thought. A well-known clowning story is 'The Clown of God'. It is a folk tale that comes in many guises. There is a Christian organization of clowns that is often present at Christian gatherings. (For further information about Christian clowns contact roly.bain@holyfool.freeserve.co.uk.) It is possible to dress in clown gear but the activities associated with clowning are just as effective: for example, slapstick humour, doing the unexpected, using balloons, bubbles, foam, water or some other messy substance. Find pupils and teachers who are willing to play along with the fun. Use clowning tricks to introduce topics based on the concept of 'the unexpected'.

Bubbles and balloons

Balloons hold great potential for delight and humour. By drawing faces on balloons, they can become symbols for people. Inflating them can be a metaphor to illustrate the power of God.

Bubbles can be used to lead into prayer or guided thinking. As they float in the air, pupils can observe the colours and be delighted by them.

Act of Worship 1
Do not judge too quickly

Introduction to theme and its purpose

In this act of worship the serious problem of the consequences of quick and damning judgements can be met in a humorous way. Being judgemental is something that everyone does; it creates needless conflict situations in any community and may lead to injustice. The use of a mislabelled food tin is highly visual, engages the sensibilities of the participants and evokes a response.

Background

Injustice is an important issue addressed by many religious and moral viewpoints. People of religious faith believe that a world that is unjust is fundamentally wrong; this is not the way God intends things to be. Jews believe God is just, in spite of all that is wrong in the world. Christians know God through Jesus, who suffered injustice; Hindus point to the process of Karma, which ultimately ensures that each individual receives just deserts; Buddhists see life as unsatisfactory if it is motivated by greed and selfishness. Humanists believe injustice is wrong because it prevents individuals from achieving full humanity.

There are several examples of Jesus' teaching on recognizing our own faults before condemning others. The focus for this act of worship is found in Luke 6.37-42. Another example is the story of the woman who has allegedly committed adultery (John 8.2-11), where Jesus asks the one without sin to cast the first stone. There may well have been a situation in school, or in current affairs, that could be used to illustrate the theme.

Preparation

Buy a tin of stewing steak, in a tin with a ring pull. Exchange the label with one from a tin of dog food.

Create a focus using a shopping bag containing the tin.

Suggested approach

Set the scene . . .

It's been a difficult morning. Pace up and down; keep looking at your watch. You are rushed and distracted at the beginning of the worship.

Describe your difficult morning. You could say something like this: You were late to bed and forgot to set the alarm. The neighbours' dog, that you've been looking after, woke you in the night.

Then you went out to the car and there was a flat tyre. Just as you were leaving for work, your partner/child reminded you to get some more food for the dog. You stopped off at the shop on the way to school to do this and arrived at school late. There has been no time for breakfast and so you are really hungry.

Then pause, look at the supposed tin of dog food (stewing meat with wrong label) and say you are SO hungry that you might just be tempted . . .

Open the tin of dog food and make a big thing of smelling it. Read the label to the pupils: tasty meat, full of vitamins and goodness, and so on. Eat some of the meat and appear to enjoy it.

Then, offer it to the Head or other teachers. No doubt they will refuse!

Then tell the pupils how you swapped the labels.

Raise the question, 'Would you now be willing to try the meat knowing the full and correct details about what is in the tin?'

Explore how we often think things, or people, are nasty without knowing much about them. We often do not go to the trouble to find out more about them.

Does this situation remind the pupils of any situations they have experienced?

Relate their responses to the advice Jesus gave in Luke 6.41-42 (taking a 'log' from your own eye before removing a 'speck' from your neighbour's). Use this as a Bible reading or retell the story in your own words. Retelling it gives the opportunity to be light-hearted and to bring out the humour in the story.

Prayer

> I thank you Lord
> for knowing me better than I know myself
> and for letting me know myself better than others know me.
> Make me, I ask you then, better than others know me.
> Make me, I ask you then, better than they suppose,
> and forgive me for what they do not know.
> Amen.

Hymn

'Give me oil in my lamp, keep me burning', No. 43 in *Come and Praise 1*, BBC Education, 1978, ISBN 0 563 32067 2.

Music

Ben King, 'Stand by me'.

James Taylor, 'You've got a friend'.

Act of Worship 2
What a laugh!

Introduction to the theme and its purpose

We are all precious as human beings and have a contribution to make. This can often be through humour and by making others smile and laugh. We can all make life happier for others; laughter is part of being human.

Background

This worship has the potential for use in a wide range of themes that explore the importance of valuing others, community, or the ways we use our talents.

The world's religions focus, in their teaching, on the importance of valuing each other. In Christianity, the teaching and example of Jesus is primarily about giving dignity to people whom others despise, or simply ignore. He touched lepers, had children brought to him, spoke to the Samaritan woman and recognized that it is part of being human to make mistakes. This he must have done with a smile. He also used humour in his storytelling; imagine the laughter raised at the thought of a camel passing through the eye of a needle!

Preparation

Prepare the room so that it is attractive for worship. Create a focal point made up of artefacts that indicate the 'fun' side of the life of the worship leader: for example, a garden spade, guitar, golf club and poetry book.

You will also need:

- a flip chart/ blank overhead transparency and pens for use during the course of the worship;
- a member of staff willing to participate by sharing their 'fun' activities (try to find a colleague with very different interests from your own);
- the image called 'The Laughing Christ' reproduced on an overhead transparency (see p. 75).

Suggested approach

Talk about the things that you enjoy doing and find fun. Ask the children to guess from the artefacts you have brought to display. Record a list on the flip chart or overhead transparency.

Ask a volunteer member of staff to record their 'fun' activities, so there is a view of two contrasting people. Bring out the humour in the different ways in which you spend your 'fun' time.

Broaden the discussion by asking volunteers from among the children to tell everyone about the things they like doing that bring fun and happiness.

Use a big bag of hats and invite volunteers to wear one that is appropriate to the 'fun' things in their life: for example, a skiing hat, a baseball hat, a woolly winter hat, a jester's hat. Encourage teachers to get involved – always a source of laughter for pupils!

Make the point that although we are all different and all have different talents, happiness can be achieved in many ways. We can also bring fun and laughter to others; it is like a giving them a gift.

At this point sing the hymn 'The best gift I can offer' (see music section).

Project the image 'The Laughing Christ'. Using this as a discussion starter, explore the ways Jesus and his disciples would have had fun together. Emphasize the fact that the 13 of them were living and travelling together for three years, so they must have known one another very well. They all had different personalities but, despite the hard times, they must also have had a lot of fun together.

Think about some of these questions:

- Is it surprising to see Jesus laughing?
- How is Jesus often shown in drawings and paintings?
- Do you think Jesus had a sense of humour?
- How do you think Jesus had fun?

Prayer/reflection

Leave the image on the screen as a focus for the time of reflection.

Use these words to guide the reflection:

> Let us, in the quietness, think of the particular gift of laughter that we have.
> (*Pause*)
> Think of how it gives us pleasure.
> (*Pause*)
> Think of how we give other people pleasure and make their lives happier.
> (*Pause*)
> Let us say thank you to God for making us each so special and with our own particular gifts.
> (*Pause*)
> Let us say thank you to God for everyone in our school with their different, special kinds of fun and humour.

Music

'The best gift I can offer', No. 59 in *Come and Praise 1,* BBC Education, 1978, ISBN 0 563 32067 2.

Use the musical talents of the staff and/or pupils for the entrance and exit music for this act of worship.

Act of Worship 3
A modern parable

Introduction to the theme

This act of worship takes as its focus the Parables of Jesus. It aims to reinforce pupils' feelings of self-worth, and illustrates that there is always the possibility to make changes in our lives.

Background

The love of God and the power it has to change lives through the Holy Spirit is an important concept within Christianity. Christians believe it is the realization of this love that is key to the transformation. There are many real-life stories that illustrate this. Nicky Cruz, who was a gangster in New York in the 1950s, became a Christian when he accepted that God could love him. He eventually became a pastor and worked with teenagers in difficult circumstances. This kind of momentous change does happen, but for the majority of people, change is a slow, gradual process as they learn more about themselves and others, through reading and experiences of life.

Preparation

Before you begin, you need five balloons in a bag. Practise blowing them up and then letting them down again. One is a spare, in case of bursts, and the fourth one you use should be pink or yellow.

You also need a permanent black marker. Have some fun as you use the balloons.

Read through the worship leader's suggested 'script' below. Feel comfortable with the words; make adjustments to your own style of presentation.

Suggested approach

If Jesus wanted people to know that God loved them, he didn't give them lessons, like we do at school. He didn't say, 'From now until playtime it's "The Love of God". Get out your green books.' He didn't give homework, either. He didn't say, 'Write me four pages on "The Love of God" by Thursday.'

No, if Jesus wanted people to know that they were important to God, he told them stories: simple stories, entertaining stories, stories with a meaning; and if you could understand the story, you could understand the meaning. We call these stories Parables, and some people think they are stories for children. They're not. They are stories for everybody – it's just that sometimes children understand them better than grown-ups.

They were stories about people and the things they were familiar with. Some of Jesus' listeners were farmers, and so he told a story about a man planting seed, and what happened to the seed. He told a story about a housewife who lost a valuable coin (worth about £50!) who turned the house upside-down until she found it. He told a story about a young man who was bored at home, and what happened to him when he went to the city looking for excitement.

But if Jesus came back *today* – if *he* were doing this act of worship, and not me – he wouldn't tell *those* stories. How many people here live on a farm? How many have relatives who are deep-sea fishermen? How many people here live in a city? (Make adjustments according to your school's context.) So those stories would be no good here.

Instead, he would tell a story that we could understand. Like this: Once upon a time there was a man who wanted to give a party for his friends. So he got a bin, and went around the house picking up all the old newspapers, and crisp packets, and sweet papers he could find. Then he got out the vacuum cleaner, and cleaned the whole house from top to bottom. Then he went to the supermarket and bought all the things to eat and drink he thought his friends would like. Then he washed all the cups and saucers and plates and knives and forks and dishes and glasses, and dried them and polished them.

And then, he thought he was ready. But, when he looked around the room, he thought, 'It doesn't look very party-like. What can I do? I know, I'll put up some balloons.' So he got a packet of balloons. (Take out the bag of balloons.) He took a balloon, and took a deep breath, and blew. (Hold the neck of this balloon firmly closed between your finger and thumb, so it will not blow up.) But nothing happened. So he took a bigger breath, and blew harder. (Repeat.) So he took an enormous breath, and blew so hard he nearly fainted – but *still* nothing happened. The balloon would *not* blow up. And then he thought, 'There are people like that. When you tell them God loves them, they will not listen, they don't want to know – so nothing ever goes in, and they never change. They stay exactly the same as before.' (Discard balloon.)

Then he took another balloon (take the second balloon), took a deep breath, and blew. (Blow up the balloon, but do not tie a knot; just hold the neck with your finger and thumb.) Before he could tie a knot in it, the balloon escaped (let balloon go) and shot around the room. And he thought, 'There are people like *that,* too. When you tell them God loves them, they *want* to know, but they can't remember from one minute to the next. Straight away, what you've told them is forgotten, and they end up just the same as they always were.'

Then he took another balloon, took a deep breath, and blew. (Blow up the third balloon.) He tied a knot in this balloon (just pretend to tie a knot and hold the balloon as before) but he couldn't have tied a very good knot, because, as time went on, the air in the balloon leaked away (let the air slowly out of the balloon as you speak) and soon all the air had gone. And he thought 'There are people just the same as *that* balloon. When you tell them God loves them, they really want to believe it but they have so many problems and worries crowding into their minds that what you tell them about God hasn't got a chance. In time, it all leaks away, and they end up just the same. There's no change.'

Then he took another balloon, took a deep breath, and blew. (This is the pink or yellow balloon. Blow it up, and tie the neck.) *This* balloon blew up and stayed up. You could see the change straight away – and the balloon stayed changed. And he thought, 'That's like the people who listen when you tell them how much God loves them. They understand, and they change. And you can see the change in them. (Take the marker and, as you say the next bit, draw eyes and a smiley mouth on the balloon.) And because they know that God loves them – they are the happiest people you will ever meet.'

Music
'Albatross' by Fleetwood Mac.

Hymn
'Our Father who art in heaven', No. 51 in *Come and Praise 1,* BBC Education, 1978, ISBN 0 563 32067 2.

Be Humorous: OHT for Act of Worship 2

Be Humorous: OHT for Act of Worship 3

Something to think about

Be Humorous

■ For Christians, worship is often a joyful experience. Identify ways in which this joy may be expressed in school worship. Is humour a feature of our school? Where is laughter most likely to be heard? In what appropriate ways might this be developed? How can humour add to the quality of worship in our school?

■ Is the setting and ethos of our worship conducive to fun? What would be necessary to create a light-hearted, comfortable but respectful atmosphere so that humour could be used?

■ List the kind of props that can enable fun to happen easily. How might they be acquired and stored?

■ Suggest techniques and skills necessary for a leader of worship to be successful in engendering a feeling of happiness, joy or well-being among pupils.

Be Multi-sensory: OHT Christian symbol – Celtic cross

6. Be Multi-sensory

Introducing the theme

There is a tendency in school to associate the Church and Christianity with teaching and learning; we should *teach* children about Christianity; they should *know* Bible stories; children should *understand* why Christians celebrate Christmas and Easter and so on. In religious education, syllabuses require that children learn *about* religion and *from* religion. This inevitably places an emphasis on the intellectual process of, for example, critically evaluating religious claims, and encouraging children to ask questions of religious beliefs and practices.

In collective worship, there is opportunity for pupils, and their teachers, to explore 'big' ideas about religion and human experience in a different way; to encounter the creative and thought-provoking events that good collective worship can offer. One of the ways in which collective worship can 'come alive' is when the experience engages the senses. And so, in this chapter, the challenge is *to be multi-sensory.*

Begin by taking a moment to look back on your own experience. Revisit some of your memories of the past. Such memories are often triggered by one or more of our senses: evocative sights, sounds, smells and tastes. The memories may be joyful or sad, uplifting or painful, but sensory stimuli will always bring them flooding back. For Christians, the stimulation of the senses forms an important part of individual and communal worship. Different traditions of the Church employ the senses in different ways, but Christian worship makes use of a feast of sensory stimuli. It could be, for example, visual images in stained glass; perfumed incense; uplifting music; shaking hands as the Peace is shared; the taste of bread and wine during the eucharistic meal. In some traditions, the senses are employed in approaches to worship that are focused on simplicity and stillness. In others, worship is a riot of colour, sound, taste and smell. The worldwide community of Christians (following in the footsteps of Christians over the centuries) worships in many different ways. In collective worship, using multi-sensory themes, we can introduce children to a range of experiences that offer a window onto this wealth of Christian experience.

Multi-sensory worship can take place at any time but you may wish to focus on the theme of the Senses, for example, over a week, or series of weeks. If it is appropriate for your setting, you could bring the theme to a dramatic climax by holding an act of worship in a local church. This could be for a major Christian festival.

Ways of using the theme

Using our senses

Our senses are a precious gift that we often take for granted. In collective worship, children can reflect on the preciousness of this gift and the ways in which their senses enable them to live life to the full. Our senses enable us to be aware of bad things as well as good things. It is important to raise questions about the ways in which we use, as well as misuse, our senses. How much of our surroundings do we take for granted? Are some objects, people, places, so familiar we are not even aware of them?

Sight

Christians use pictures to tell stories. Stained glass, a painting, a drawing or a photograph can be used to introduce a story, an event or a theme. Pictures also create atmosphere. This can be reflected in approaches to collective worship. When using images, ask questions like: How does this make us feel? How can our eyes be used to discover new ideas? Is seeing believing? Christian artefacts can also be used in this way. Encourage pupils to find detail in what they see; to look for signs and symbols to help them raise questions about the objects and their meaning for Christians. Explore ways of using different types of crosses, church vestments in different liturgical colours, floral decorations, candles, carvings, chalice and paten (the cup, for wine, and plate, for bread, used in Holy Communion). These can also be used as a visual focus for worship.

Sound

Christians down the centuries have spoken of the importance of talking and listening to God and to each other. Listening is the gift that we often find most emphasized by the great Christian saints and teachers. It could be listening to a piece of music, listening to a friend in need, listening to the words of the Bible, listening for the voice of God in prayer. In collective worship, try using some of the sounds used by Christians to help them worship. You could ring a bell to signal the start of worship; try chanting a psalm or a prayer as well as singing hymns and songs; listen to the sound of silence!

Smell

Our sense of smell can be extremely powerful and evocative. For the Christian Church, this sense has always been used to enhance worship in a variety of traditions. Incense, for example, is used by some Christians to focus the mind for prayer and meditation. Children often notice the smell of churches and cathedrals when they visit; it might be incense, flowers, candles, or the more down-to-earth aromas of polished wooden pews and musty old buildings! They all go together, however, to create a sense of place, of sacred space and a special atmosphere that can contribute to Christian worship.

Touch

Hands, and their many different movements, are frequently used in Christian art and symbolism: the healing hands of Jesus, the hand of God raised in judgement, hands used creatively, for good or for evil purposes. They can be used to express our feelings and they can be powerful tools in effecting change in the world. In Christian worship, hands, and the sense of touch, play a significant role in liturgy and ritual. Some of these include shaking hands when sharing the peace; the laying on of hands in confirmation and ordination; anointing the baptized with holy oil; washing feet on Maundy Thursday; and praying with hands held together.

Taste

It is perhaps not surprising that the sense of taste is so closely associated with religious worship, celebrations and festivals in many of the world's faith traditions. Food is the fuel of life and for Christians this includes spiritual food. Bread is a potent symbol running through the Bible and in John's Gospel Jesus is referred to as 'the bread of life'. The most central ritual activity, for the majority of Christians, focuses on the sacred meal, the Eucharist or Holy Communion, in which bread and wine are shared. In doing this Christians follow Jesus' commandment, 'Do this in remembrance of me.'

Sensitivity, imagination and insight

In all aspects of learning and experience, self-awareness and self-expression come through sensory alertness. Christians find God in a variety of ways and in their worship the five senses are used to sharpen their sensitivity, imagination and insight. In each act of worship, sights, sounds, tastes, touch and smell combine to create a multi-sensory experience that helps Christians to grow in their faith. Christian worship is a combination of activities that feed body, mind and spirit. In collective worship in schools, there is opportunity to use insights from the Christian tradition to model an experience that stimulates pupils' spiritual, intellectual, moral, social and cultural development.

Senses to wonder

The senses form the basis of human patterns of communication. By exploring the senses in collective worship, pupils experience the ways in which Christians try to make meaning of life's complexities. It becomes possible to understand how the sights, sounds and actions of Christianity sharpen the awareness of the believer. Children can experience for themselves ways of using their senses to wonder at the world and its people and to be open and responsive to their needs.

Act of Worship 1
A journey through Holy Week

Introduction to the theme and its purpose

This act of worship is intended for a whole-school assembly but could be adapted for other groupings. It is most effective if it can follow a programme of study, in RE, on Easter. This would enable pupils to be familiar with the key events of the Easter story. It is a multi-sensory reflection on the events that Christians mark in the rituals of Holy Week. Its purpose is to enable pupils to consider the last few days of Jesus' life and to reflect upon the Christian belief in resurrection.

Background

This act of worship is based on the idea of the Stations of the Cross and takes the form of a simple liturgy of readings, prayers and responses. There are traditionally 14 stations, or visual representations of Jesus' final journey from his trial to his death. These may be pictures or sculptures, usually located around a church building. Throughout Lent and Easter the images are used as part of the rituals and devotions of the season. Bible readings and prayers are said at each station as Christians follow the last hours of Jesus' life.

This concept of journeying through the Easter story, like a kind of mini-pilgrimage, has been taken and adapted in this act of worship to cover the events of Holy Week.

It begins with the events of Palm Sunday and ends with Easter Day. You may wish to hold the act of worship in two parts: for example, ending with the station for Good Friday before the Easter holidays and beginning the new term, after Easter, with the Easter Day station. Another possibility, weather permitting, is to hold the first part of the act of worship indoors and end with the last station outside.

Preparation

This act of worship can take place in a classroom, a school hall, a church or the school grounds.

Set up the 'stations', either around the room or down the centre of the room, using the following artefacts. Ensure they are visible for all the participants.

Station 1: palm branch or palm crosses
Station 2: a small leather bag or pouch and some coins
Station 3: a jug of water, a bowl, a white towel, bread and wine/chalice and paten
Station 4: the branch of a tree (if possible, an olive tree)
Station 5: a wooden cross
Station 6: a large rock or stone standing on a piece of cloth
Station 7: Easter (paschal) candle

Transfer the image of the cross, with the prayer response (see p. 92), to an overhead transparency and project it so that it is a focal point for all participants.

Suggested approach

Gather the pupils into the worship space. Use music to create atmosphere (see examples).

Two pupils, one to read and one to light a candle, stand at each 'station'.

Ring a bell as a signal that worship is ready to start.

Use a form of welcome, for example:

Leader   The Lord be with you.
Response   **And also with you.**

You should then explain that everyone will be making a journey together through the events of Holy Week.

Station 1

Reader 1   As we reflect on this most holy week we remember that first Palm Sunday
                when Jesus showed great humility by riding into Jerusalem on a donkey.
                The crowds welcomed him with shouts of 'Hosanna!'
                We pray that we too might show humility in our lives and like the crowds,
                welcome Jesus.

All   **We pray this as we follow in the footsteps of Jesus.**

(*A candle is lit at Station 1*)

Station 2

Reader 2   As we reflect on this most holy week we remember the day that Jesus strode
                into the Temple and in his anger threw out the greedy money-changers and
                those selling animals for sacrifice.
                We pray that like Jesus we might show anger at injustice in our world today.

All: **We pray this as we follow in the footsteps of Jesus.**

(*A candle is lit at Station 2*)

Station 3

Reader 3   As we reflect on this most holy week we remember that first Maundy Thursday when Jesus washed his disciples' feet. Jesus shared the Passover meal with his friends and asked them to remember him whenever they shared bread and wine. We pray that we might care for others and always remember Jesus when we worship together.

All   **We pray this as we follow in the footsteps of Jesus.**

(A candle is lit at Station 3)

Station 4

Reader 4   As we reflect on this most holy week we remember the garden of Gethsemane when Jesus prayed as the disciples slept. We remember too how Judas betrayed Jesus with a kiss and handed him over for arrest.

       We pray we will always turn to you in prayer. Help us to be loyal to our friends.

All   **We pray this as we follow in the footsteps of Jesus.**

(A candle is lit at Station 4)

Station 5

Reader 5   As we reflect on this most holy week we remember that first Good Friday when Jesus was brought before Pontius Pilate and condemned to a very cruel death. We remember Jesus' words from the cross: 'Father, forgive them, for they know not what they do.' We pray that like Jesus we may have compassion to forgive.

All   **We pray this as we follow in the footsteps of Jesus.**

(A candle is lit at Station 5)

Station 6

Reader 6   As we reflect on this most holy week we remember that first Easter Saturday when Jesus' body lay in the darkness of a stone tomb. We remember his mother Mary and his friends who were with Jesus when he died. We pray for all those who mourn the death of a loved one, that they too might receive comfort in their hours of darkness.

All   **We pray this as we follow in the footsteps of Jesus.**

(A candle is lit at Station 6)

Station 7

Reader 7 As we reflect on this most holy week we remember that first Easter day when Jesus' friends discovered the empty tomb and realized that he had risen from the dead. We share with them in the joy of Easter and of the hope of new life.

We pray that this Easter joy will remain with us and our loved ones throughout all our lives.

All   **We pray this in the footsteps of Jesus.**

(*A candle is lit at Station 7*)

Bring the act of worship to a close by singing an Easter hymn or song.

As the children leave, play music (see example below).

Music

As the children gather for worship:
Allegri, 'Miserere Mei'.
Franck, 'Panis Angelicus'.

Bach, *St Matthew Passion,* for example No. 78, the final chorus of Part 2.
Lloyd-Webber, 'Pie Jesu' from *Requiem*.

As the children leave:
Handel, 'Hallelujah Chorus' from *Messiah*.

Act of Worship 2
Follow the star

Introduction to the theme and its purpose

Epiphany is the part of the Christmas cycle that can sometimes be overlooked. The Feast of Epiphany falls on 6 January. This act of worship could be used at the beginning of the new school term. It presents the themes of journeying and gift-giving through the words of the traditional hymn 'We three kings'.

Background

Epiphany is the final phase of the Christmas cycle of the Church year. In the Orthodox Church it is the day on which the birth of Jesus is celebrated. The word 'Epiphany' means 'showing forth' and marks the visit of the Magi (or Wise Men) to see Jesus. In the biblical account (Matthew 2.1-12) the Magi are described as travellers coming from the East. The significance of this is that they were the first non-Jews to pay homage to Jesus, reflecting the importance of the birth of Jesus for all people. The Gospel account does not identify the number of Magi, or their names, but over the years, in traditional legend and story, they have become known as the Three Kings: Caspar, Melchior and Balthazar.

There is an old Polish custom of the priest blessing pieces of chalk at Epiphany. These are used to mark the doorways of houses with the numerals for the New Year separated by the initials of the Magi: so, for example, in 2005 this would read '20+C+M+B+05'. Houses are marked and blessed to signify that a welcome would be found there, just in case the Magi should be passing. And that welcome is extended for all travellers and pilgrims.

Preparation

A nativity set in a prominent place on view to all. You will need:

- figures of Mary, Joseph, Jesus and the shepherds (figures for the three Magi will be added during the worship);

- a large gold star;

- the words of the song 'We Three Kings' on an overhead transparency (see 'Suggested approach' and 'Music' below) and the picture from p. 93;

- a pen to write the appropriate numbers for the calendar year onto the picture;

- three boxes to represent the Magi's gifts, wrapped in bright, shiny paper. One should be gold colour.

To create atmosphere, warm a mixture of oil of frankincense or myrrh (obtained from chemists and health-food stores) in an aromatherapy burner. Frankincense and myrrh can also be purchased in granular form to be burned over charcoal. Someone from your local church may be able to demonstrate this for you.

You will also need to organize three classes or groups of children to sing the verses of the song (one to sing Caspar's verse, one Melchior's verse, and one Balthazar's verse).

Suggested approach

Introduce pupils to the Feast of the Epiphany: Christmas is not over yet; a special journey is to be made, with the Magi, to bring gifts for the baby Jesus.

Talk about the journeys pupils have made, whether long or short. Focus upon the preparation for long journeys, and the need to know what route to follow. The Magi did not use a map for their journey; they followed the stars.

All sing:

> We three kings of Orient are;
> bearing gifts we traverse afar;
> field and fountain,
> moor and mountain,
> following yonder star.

Chorus:

> O star of wonder, star of night,
> star with royal beauty bright;
> westward leading, still proceeding,
> guide us to thy perfect light.

During the singing, a pupil or pupils remove the shepherds from the nativity scene and another pupil brings a large gold star and places it above the stable.

The 'Melchior' group sings:

> Born a King on Bethlehem plain,
> gold I bring to crown him again,
> King for ever, ceasing never,
> over us all to reign.

All sing the chorus.

During this verse, a pupil brings one of the Magi figures and places it in the nativity scene. Another pupil brings the gift representing gold.

The 'Caspar' group sings:

> Frankincense to offer have I,
> incense owns a Deity nigh,
> prayer and praising gladly raising,
> worship him, God most high.

All sing the chorus.

During this verse, a pupil brings the second of the Magi figures and places it in the nativity scene. Another pupil brings the gift representing frankincense.

The 'Balthazar' group sings:

>Myrrh is mine, its bitter perfume
>breathes a life of gathering gloom;
>sorrowing, sighing, bleeding, dying,
>sealed in the stone-cold tomb.

All sing the chorus:

During this verse, a pupil brings the third of the Magi figures and places it in the nativity scene. Another pupil brings the gift representing myrrh.

All sing:

>Glorious now, behold him arise,
>King and God and sacrifice;
>alleluia, alleluia,
>earth to heaven replies.
>
>O star of wonder, star of night,
>star with royal beauty bright;
>westward leading, still proceeding,
>guide us to thy perfect light.

Project the picture from p. 93 and explain the Polish Christian custom of house blessing (see 'Background' above). On the overhead transparency, fill in the appropriate number for the new calendar year.

Prayer

Use the picture as the focus for prayer and reflection.

>Loving God,
>travel with us in this year ahead.
>Bless our school
>and help us to make it a place where all are welcome.
>Amen.

Music

'We three kings of Orient are', words and music by J. H. Hopkins, No. 570 in *Hymns Old and New*, Kevin Mayhew Ltd, 1988, ISBN 0 86209 071 7.

Act of Worship 3
A Harvest rainbow

Introduction to the theme and its purpose

A traditional legend is used in this act of worship to illustrate the responsibilities we all hold for the natural world and for each other. This challenges us to explore the ways in which we all use our gifts and talents to share the world's resources and to work for justice. The richness of bright colours is used to create a visual impact when they are united in the Harvest rainbow as a symbol of hope through unity and peace.

Background

Harvest is traditionally a time for giving thanks for all the fruits of the earth. While not officially a festival in the Christian calendar, virtually all churches and schools set aside a time in early autumn to mark the occasion. As well as focusing on the beauty and abundance of the earth, it is a time when Christians are reminded of their responsibilities as caretakers of God's creation. It is a challenging thought that though only 20 per cent of people live in developed countries, they consume 53 per cent of the world's energy; they eat 44 per cent of the world's meat; and they own about 80 per cent of the world's motor vehicles. (See Yann Arthus-Bertrand, *The Earth from the Air*, Thames & Hudson, 2003, ISBN 0 500 54278 3.)

Archbishop Desmond Tutu often used the traditional legend of the Rainbow People when campaigning for justice and freedom in South Africa.

Preparation

Prepare some, or all, of the pupils with ribbons, or pieces of fabric, in blue, red, green or yellow.

Place a focus table in a central position. Cover it in a brightly coloured cloth, with a Bible open at the Genesis reading (reference given below).

Find or make a large picture of a rainbow, and display prominently.

Make an overhead transparency of the picture on p. 94 (OHT for Act of Worship 3) to project during the reflection time.

Reading

Genesis 1.27-31.

Suggested approach

Welcome the pupils with a traditional greeting, for example:

Leader	The Lord be with you.
All	**And also with you.**

Introduce the Harvest theme and explain that everyone has an important role to play; they are part of the Harvest Rainbow.

Invite a pupil to read from the Bible Genesis 1.27-31.

Introduce the Legend of the Rainbow People:

At Harvest time Christians remember the story of creation and think about how they can care for the world's resources and look after each other. Archbishop Desmond Tutu is a famous Christian priest who has spent his whole life campaigning for justice and freedom in South Africa and other parts of the world. He often tells this traditional legend to make us think about how we can use our gifts to help others and share the world's resources more equally.

Invite the pupils to listen carefully as the story unfolds; they will hear the names of the special colours they are representing. Whenever their colour is mentioned, they stand up and wave their colours for everyone to see.

The legend of the Rainbow People

God loved his people whom he had filled with life. They began to look at each other, to speak to each other, to care about each other. As they explored their world they found coloured ribbons lying on the ground. They were excited and ran about collecting them up. Some chose blue (*pause as the pupils representing the Blue group stand up, wave their colour, then sit again*), some red (*pause as before*), some green (*pause*), some yellow (*pause*). They enjoyed tying the ribbons round each other and laughing.

Suddenly, a cold wind blew; it made them shiver. They looked at each other, realized they looked different and stopped trusting each other. Each colour gathered together, the blues in one corner (*pause, as before*), the reds in another corner (*pause*), the greens in a third corner (*pause*) and the yellows into a fourth corner (*pause*). They forgot they had been friends and cared for each other. They built walls to separate themselves and keep the others out. But they found that the reds (*pause*) had water, but no food; the blues (*pause*) had food but no water; the greens (*pause*) had twigs to make fires, but no shelter; and the yellows (*pause*) had shelter but nothing to keep them warm.

After a long time of misery one of them, remembering God's creation, said loudly, 'Come out everybody, what are you afraid of? Let's talk to each other and tell each other about what we have to give and what we are in need of.'

The people peeped out and slowly came out together. 'Why don't we put together what we have and share it?' They started to talk and they realized that they liked each other. They knocked down the walls and welcomed each other as old friends.

When they realized the colours had divided them, they wanted to throw them away. But they knew that they would miss the richness of the bright colours. So instead they mixed the colours to make a beautiful rainbow ribbon (*refer to your rainbow image*) and it became their symbol of unity and peace.

Reflection

Light a candle.

Project the picture from p. 94 alongside the rainbow image. Use these images as a stimulus for reflecting together about the legend. You could use questions like these:

> I wonder which part of this story is most about us?
>
> I wonder where you are in this picture/these pictures?
>
> I wonder how we build walls around ourselves?
>
> I wonder how we can be rainbow people?

Prayer

> Heavenly Father, at this harvest time
>
> we thank you for the beauty of the earth
>
> and for the gifts we have been given.
>
> Help us to be rainbow people,
>
> to work for justice and peace,
>
> to bring people together
>
> and to share all we have.
>
> Amen.

Music

Music for entering and leaving:

The setting of 'All things Bright and Beautiful', from the CD called *Gloria: the Sacred Music of John Rutter*, Collegium, 1998.

Harvest songs:

Nos 133–9 in *Come and Praise 2*, BBC Education, 1988, ISBN 0 563 34247 1.

We pray this as we follow
in the footsteps of Jesus

20+C+M+B+

The Rainbow People

Be Multi-sensory: OHT for Act of Worship 3

Something to think about

Be Multi-sensory

■ For Christians, worship is a multi-sensory experience. Identify ways in which Christian worship engages body, mind and spirit.

■ How could acts of worship on the theme of 'The Senses' be incorporated into our school's worship programme

> Over a week
>
> Or over a half term
>
> Or to coincide with Church festivals?

■ How could all acts of worship in our school become more multi-sensory?

■ Make a list of multi-sensory artefacts that could be used as a resource for school worship. Start to collect these together. How could children be involved in using these objects to create a worship table?

■ Collect posters and pictures that could be used as a focus for worship. In groups, devise questions to be used, with the images, as a stimulus for imaginative discussion for example:

> What is your favourite part of this picture?
>
> What part of this picture is most important?
>
> What part of this picture could we take away and still have all the picture we need?

Be Multi-sensory: OHT for training

Be in Communion: OHT Christian symbol – bread and wine

7. Be in Communion

Introducing the theme

The Eucharist (Greek for 'thanksgiving'), or Holy Communion lies at the heart of Anglican worship. Church of England schools play a significant role in the Anglican community and some of them choose to mark their distinctive place by offering eucharistic worship. Holding a school Eucharist, however, is not a requirement! There may be very good reasons why the school chooses not to offer it. Deciding this is usually done in partnership with local clergy. In this chapter, the experiences of a range of Church schools are shared, and some of the issues they have encountered are explored.

The complexities of rules and regulations concerning children and Holy Communion, and the great variety in practice in dioceses in different parts of the country, have been reason enough for many schools to decide to avoid the issue. One concern that is often voiced centres on the admission of children to Holy Communion. In churches, children receive the elements (bread and wine) only when they have been either admitted to Communion (usually around age seven and following a short course of preparation) or confirmed. Therefore, many primary-school children taking part in a school Eucharist are perceived as being 'excluded' from receiving communion.

So how have schools that have chosen to celebrate the Eucharist worked through this issue? They argue that, if the service is viewed as a whole, pupils still may be very much involved. Even if they cannot receive the elements, they can feel a very real sense of belonging and know that the Eucharist is a special occasion. In some schools, children come up either individually or class by class to receive a blessing. They are able to listen and watch as teachers and non-teaching staff, governors, parents and visitors receive communion. Pupils can be involved in the planning of the Eucharist and be responsible for various parts of the liturgy: for example, in presenting a piece of drama, playing musical instruments, writing and reading prayers. Some clergy encourage pupils to mirror their liturgical actions. Pupils can act as crucifer and acolytes and can assist the celebrant. They can be 'welcomers', prepare the school hall or church, make the bread, bake cakes or biscuits to be served after the service, escort visitors and so on.

The Eucharist can be a high point of a school's worship programme, whether it takes place weekly, termly, or annually. There are many and diverse ways to explore this form of worship, but for schools that choose to do so, the experience is widely recognized for the significant contribution it makes to the life of the whole school community.

Ways of using the theme

The hub of the wheel

St Thomas of Canterbury Voluntary Aided Infant School in the Diocese of Chelmsford holds a school Eucharist once a term. Here very young children are involved in eucharistic worship. Barbara Stringer, the headteacher, explains that the Eucharist is the foundation of the school.

> It is where we start. We needed to go deeper than assembly and felt the children were ready for this. Sharing a meal is something they experience both at home and at school. It is also at the heart of religious celebrations within many faith traditions. The service at St Thomas's tries to draw on the children's own experiences of sharing food and relates this to its centrality for the Christian faith. It's the hub of the wheel and it makes this school a very special place.

St Thomas's incumbent, Father Bob White, works closely with the headteacher in planning the worship. They believe the Eucharist grows out of and reflects the events in the school, rather than becoming an 'add-on' to the worship programme. Services are carefully planned to follow the pattern of the liturgy. Their approach is 'Keep it simple, but allow it to grow and evolve and give everyone a chance to grow within it'. At the Harvest Eucharist the children each take a piece of blessed bread and eat it as they leave the worship and go out into the life of the school.

Lunchtime Eucharist

Could you transform your school library, or another room, into a chapel once a week to celebrate a lunchtime Eucharist? This happens at St Mary and All Saints School, Reading, where children are admitted to first communion at age seven. In this voluntary aided primary school, the incumbent is a regular visitor and is actively involved in all aspects of the life of the school. On Wednesday lunchtimes, pupils join him, voluntarily, to share in the Eucharist.

Experiencing sacramental worship

Pupils in both voluntary aided and voluntary controlled schools should have the opportunity to explore the Eucharist as part of their RE curriculum. The experience of participating in a school Eucharist, however, can deepen pupils' understanding of this central act of Christian worship.

> We aim to give the children experience of sacramental worship at a level which they can understand and in which they can participate. Seeing adults from the community and the staff make their communion conveys the fact that Christian practice is for adults as well as children. The connections made with the curriculum and the Church's year imply that the things of the spirit are integral to everyday life and that Christians are part of a worldwide faith community

The Revd Neil Crawford-Jones, Chair of Governors of Romsey Abbey Primary School

Agape meals

Some schools have decided to celebrate the Eucharist in the form of an agape meal (the word literally means 'love feast'). This takes the form of a shared meal where bread is blessed and eaten. In the Early Church the Communion service would have been very much part of an everyday shared meal where everyone would have brought along something to eat.

Liturgies

There are both challenges and possibilities in using set Church of England liturgies for a school Eucharist. *Common Worship* offers considerable choice. A Service of the Word with a Celebration of Holy Communion (*Common Worship* main volume, p. 25) offers the most flexibility. Guidance on planning such a service may be found on pages 21–3 of *New Patterns for Worship* (see Resources list).

Within this service, authorized texts must be used for the Confession and Absolution, the Collect and the Eucharistic Prayer. Most of the texts currently authorized for use may be found in the *Common Worship* main volume. The authorized Confessions and Absolutions are conveniently collected together on pages 81–97 of *New Patterns for Worship*.

There are eight Eucharistic Prayers which may be used. Of these, Prayer H is the shortest. Others favour Prayers D (which was designed with children in mind), E (the briefest of the four Eucharistic Prayers which follow the traditional Western pattern) or G. Short proper prefaces may be added to Prayers A, B and C, and these may be specially composed (provided that they balance the style and overall length of the rest of the prayer).

For other parts of the services, the priest is given a degree of discretion in the selection of suitable texts (see notes to the service, *Common Worship* main volume, p. 26).

Act of Worship 1
A Eucharist day

Glenis Taylor, headteacher of Baines Endowed Church of England Primary School, Blackpool, decided to involve the whole school in the preparation of a School Eucharist. Here she describes how, and why, they went about this new school venture.

The almost simultaneous appointment to a parish of a new incumbent and a new Deacon with the appointment to its primary school of new headteacher is a real recipe for engendering reflection on, and consequent development of, the Christian character and ethos of the school. From our reflections we determined that fundamental to such development was that our pupils and our staff including myself, should come to a greater understanding of the features of the Eucharist Service, their symbolism and relevance to our lives today.

Starting from the principle that primary children learn best when they are fully involved in creating their own learning we planned a day's activities which began with workshop activities and ended with every child being involved in a demonstration of what they had learned in a celebration of the Eucharistic Service. This was no mean feat, with eight classes totalling 280 children aged seven to eleven!

Our church deacon was our major source of ideas in our initial planning, but we also enlisted the support of a diocesan adviser. We decided on our overall theme of 'Jesus changes lives', taking the experiences and work of St Paul as our biblical focus. We drew up our draft proposals for the component parts of the service and how they might be developed into experiences for the children. These were then discussed and modified in a meeting with all teaching staff. Each member of staff opted to lead a workshop of their choosing and we enlisted the help of a diocesan adviser, church members, parents and even one of our cleaners to lead other workshops. Each workshop leader was responsible for gathering together the resources they needed; the school worship budget was the source of funding.

When the appointed day dawned, we utilized every inch of space for the morning's workshops. Classroom furniture had been stacked in corners so that there was enough space for groups to develop their music, drama, poetry, dance and readings. The hall had to be precisely time-tabled for the morning to give each of these groups the opportunity to practice in situ. Other groups needed space for clay work, embroidery, appliqué, and paper chain making. The school was a proverbial hive of activity with small groups in corridors, stock-rooms, the staff-room and the library. It turned out to be a gloriously sunny day so we even had a group working on their appliqué crosses in our quad garden. Adding to the atmosphere, the smell of freshly baking bread in one classroom pervaded the whole school. The morning was a very rewarding experience in itself; over the lunch-break staff talked about the children's sense of pride in what they had produced, their obvious growth in understanding of, for example the symbolism of flowers in church, the types of prayer in services, etc. There was a tremendous feeling in school of working together to produce something very, very special. This feeling came really came alive in the afternoon as our Eucharist Service proved to be a very special experience for us all.

Every item used in the service had been created by our children; in their groups they had discussed the meaning behind it, the symbolism of it and its use. Their understanding and their real involvement shone through as children processed in with the altar cloth they had printed, the flowers they had arranged, the paten and candlesticks they had formed. The delight in the faces of the children who had made the vicar's cope was clear for all to see. As the service continued children danced to portray Jesus' light changing lives, dramatized Paul in prison, recited their poems about incarceration and release and prayed their prayers that Paul's work, to take Jesus' message, should be continued by us, so that it can continue to change people's lives.

The choir created an atmosphere of sanctity and calm as communion was being taken and, although there were no children in school at that time who could take communion with us, their real involvement was evident in their quietness and obvious concentration.

The workshop day was one of the highlights of my first year at the school and I feel it has been a major factor in our school's development. It resulted in a deeper understanding of the Eucharist in children and in staff, including myself. But the impact was wider than this. It enhanced our understanding of the importance of spiritual development in the children, in ourselves and in our whole school community. It gave us a real understanding of what the ethos of a Church school really feels like in practice, and the determination and insight to continue to develop this.

Act of Worship 2
Holy Communion

Guidelines for devising a school Eucharist

The following is an example of a liturgy for a school Eucharist with notes for guidance, and has been devised in consultation with the Secretary to the Church of England's Liturgical Commission.

The structure is based on that given in *Common Worship*, p. 25 (see guidance given in the paragraph on Liturgies, p. 99). Guidance notes are indicated by ●

The Gathering

We ask God to be with us

Priest   The Lord be with you

All   **and also with you.**

All   **Holy Father, you know all our secret thoughts.**
    Help us to keep our minds fixed on you.
    In Jesus' name we pray. Amen

Confession

● Authorized forms of confession and absolution may be found in the *Book of Common Prayer*, in the services and on pages 122–37 of *Common Worship* and on pages 81-97 of *New Patterns for Worship*. The priest (or another minister) may introduce the confession with suitable words, e.g. 'Now we are going to say sorry to God'. In the following example, a Kyrie confession is used. This allows for the insertion of short sentences between the petitions of the Kyrie, suitable for particular seasons or themes. A selection of suitable Kyrie confessions may be found in *Common Worship*, pp. 133–4, and *New Patterns for Worship*, pp. 91–4.

We have not always worshipped God, our creator.

Lord, have mercy.

Lord, have mercy.

We have not always followed Christ, our Saviour.

Christ, have mercy.

Christ, have mercy.

We have not always trusted in the Spirit, our guide.

Lord, have mercy.

Lord, have mercy.

Absolution

● An authorized form should be used. This example is B74 in *New Patterns for Worship*, p. 96.

Priest   May almighty God have mercy on us,

forgive us our sins,

and bring us to everlasting life,

through Jesus Christ our Lord.

Amen.

Prayer for the day: The Collect

● An authorized collect should be used. In addition to those in *Common Worship*, a new set of contemporary language collects has recently been made available: *Additional Collects*, Church House Publishing, 2004.

Listening to God's word

Bible readings

● There should be two Bible readings, one being a Gospel reading. These can of course be short and may be dramatized, sung or read responsively. *The Dramatised Bible* is a helpful resource (see Resources list).

Short talk

● This could also be presented in a variety of ways: for example, using drama, interviews, discussion and audio-visual aids.

What we believe

We believe in one God who made the world and all that is in it.

We believe in Jesus Christ, our Saviour, who died to save us all.

We believe in the Holy Spirit sent by God to help us.

We believe in the promise of a new life now and when this one is over.

We believe we are forgiven because God's promises are never broken. Amen.

Prayers

When the person leading the prayers says: Lord in your mercy

All reply: Hear our prayer.

The Peace

Priest   The peace of the Lord be always with you

All   **and also with you.**

The Communion

The table is prepared and bread and wine are placed upon it.

● An authorized Eucharistic prayer must be used. There are eight provided for use with Order One. Prayer H is included here.

Priest	The Lord be with you	*(or)*	The Lord is here.
All	**and also with you.**		**His Spirit is with us.**

Priest   Lift up your hearts.

All   **We lift them to the Lord.**

Priest   Let us give thanks to the Lord our God.

All   **It is right to give thanks and praise.**

Priest   It is right to praise you, Father, Lord of all creation;
in your love you made us for yourself.

When we turned away
you did not reject us,
but came to meet us in your Son.

All   **You embraced us as your children
and welcomed us to sit and eat with you.**

Priest   In Christ you shared our life
that we might live in him and he in us.

All   **He opened his arms of love upon the cross
and made for all the perfect sacrifice for sin.**

Priest   On the night he was betrayed,
at supper with his friends
he took bread, and gave you thanks;
he broke it and gave it to them, saying:
Take, eat; this is my body which is given for you;
do this in remembrance of me.

All   **Father, we do this in remembrance of him:
his body is the bread of life.**

Priest   At the end of supper, taking the cup of wine,
he gave you thanks, and said:
Drink this, all of you; this is my blood of the new covenant,
which is shed for you for the forgiveness of sins;
do this in remembrance of me.

| All | **Father, we do this in remembrance of him:** |
| | **his blood is shed for all.** |

Priest	As we proclaim his death and celebrate his rising in glory,
	send your Holy Spirit that this bread and this wine
	may be to us the body and blood of your dear Son.

| All | **As we eat and drink these holy gifts** |
| | **make us one in Christ, our risen Lord.** |

Priest	With your whole Church throughout the world
	we offer you this sacrifice of praise
	and lift our voice to join the eternal song of heaven:

All	**Holy, holy, holy Lord,**
	God of power and might,
	Heaven and earth are full of your glory.
	Hosanna in the highest.

The Lord's Prayer is said.

The priest breaks the consecrated bread.

Invitation to communion: The priest invites everyone to come forward.

After communion

● It is not necessary to use an authorized post communion prayer. The following example is taken from *New Patterns for Worship*, p. 362.

Lord,
we have broken your bread
and received your life.
By the power of your Spirit
keep us always in your love
through Jesus Christ our Lord.
Amen.

Blessing and Dismissal

The priest blesses the people and then says:

Go in peace to love and serve the Lord.

All: In the name of Christ. Amen.

School Eucharist planning sheet

Date: Location:

Time: Class/year group/whole school:

Celebrant: Theme:

Worship order	What's involved	Who does it
Music to enter		
Gathering song		
Greeting		
'Saying sorry' rite		
Prayers		
Reading/drama		
Talk		
Intercessions		
The Peace		
Offertory song		
Eucharistic prayer		
The Lord's Prayer		
Breaking bread		
Communion song/s		
Closing prayer		
Blessing		
Final song		
Music to depart		

Be in Communion: OHT for Act of Worship 1

Be in Communion: OHT for Act of Worship 2

Something to think about

Be in Communion

Deciding whether or not to hold a school Eucharist can, in itself, be a big decision. Take time to think through the issues, consider the benefits and hear the concerns. Consult other schools where a Eucharist is celebrated; arrange to visit and observe their practice. If you decide to go ahead . . .

1.   Who will be involved in the planning and preparation?

- the whole school, one year group
- pupils, staff, clergy, parents, governors,
- members of the church community

2.   In what way can the Eucharist become part of your programme of school worship?

- Weekly, monthly, termly
- Annually: for example, at the start or end of the school year
- Following a module of work on the Eucharist in religious education
- To coincide with church festivals

3.   Where is the best location?

- The school hall
- A classroom
- An open-air event in the school grounds
- In church

4. In consultation with clergy, decide who will receive communion.

- All present
- Only those who receive in their 'home' churches
- Staff and parents
- the Agape tradition (share bread that is blessed separately)

Be Anglican: OHT Christian symbol – Paschal candle

8. Be Anglican

Introducing the theme

The principles and practices of the Anglican Church offer a framework for the life of the Church school and this is possibly expressed most clearly in its worship. One of the things that can be distinctive about a Church school is that all the activities of the school are undergirded by worship and feed into it. It is a means by which Christian values can be reflected and affirmed and the spirituality of the pupils can find expression and development.

Most Church schools welcome pupils from different religious backgrounds as well as pupils whose families have no religious affiliation. School worship, while reflecting the Anglican tradition, should not impinge upon the integrity of pupils and the religious traditions they represent. Worship is a key player in telling the story of the school and an opportunity to bring together children and teachers from all faiths and none. Religious and cultural diversity is there to be celebrated and all can feel they have something to offer and contribute to the school family to which they belong.

Many schools are working on what it is to be a multi-faith Church school, by building strong and trusting relationships with local faith communities. Worship is an opportunity to share experience of commitment and spiritual insight. What is most important, however, is that Church schools provide a safe place for pupils to explore, however tentatively, beliefs about God and about religious commitment as expressed by people of good faith throughout the world.

So how can Anglican schools reflect some of the essential features of their tradition within their worship programme? Clearly, Church schools cannot encapsulate all of the richness of the Anglican tradition all of the time, but when planning worship it is useful to be aware of the different opportunities pupils can experience during their school life.

Ways of using the theme

Prayer

It is important to use language for prayers that is appropriate to pupils' experience and understanding. There are collections of prayers now widely available that use simple ideas and that include prayers written by children. A general rule of thumb is to use few words rather than many and, where possible, develop ease with moments of silence.

The Lord's Prayer, in either its traditional or modern form, is one of the many time-honoured prayers that can be used on a regular basis in school worship. Pupils can learn creative ways of saying, singing and signing the prayer. There are also other traditional prayers, noted for the rhythm and beauty of their language, and these can be read together or learned by heart: for example, the prayer attributed to St Francis of Assisi, and the prayers of St Patrick and St Ignatius (see p. 10, p. 62 and Appendix). More recently, Cliff Richard's Millennium Prayer has become a favourite in many schools (arranged by Paul Field, Stephen Deal, Cliff Richard, Nigel Wright and published by EMI/CMP Nashville/Cop. Con.).

Greetings

Exchange a formal liturgical greeting:

| **Leader** | The Lord be with you. |
| **All** | **And also with you.** |

or

| **Leader** | The Lord is here. |
| **All** | **His Spirit is with us.** |

Finding a regular pattern of worship

Within the Anglican Church is the tradition of participating in a regular pattern of prayer and worship, for example the Daily Office and the Eucharist. Special acts of worship are used to mark the passing of milestones throughout life, for example, baptism, marriage and death.

Church schools can also follow in the footsteps of this tradition by offering a regular pattern of worship: by following the cycle of the church year; by marking events in the child's experience, such as arriving at or leaving school, or the beginning or end of the school year. Worship is also a place to handle joys and sorrows, or to mark important national or local events. This is especially true of bereavement in the community or in the life of the nation.

The liturgical year

When planning worship, observe the cycle of the Anglican year. The major seasons, festivals and saints' days provide a structure for collective worship. The worship focus table can reflect the different times of the Church year by using different coloured cloths to denote the appropriate season, such as purple for Lent. Make connections between the colours to be seen in church and the colours used in school worship.

Liturgical clock

A liturgical clock is a visual representation of the colours and seasons of the Church year. This could be made of wood or felt and made in school or commercially. (See, for example, *The Complete Guide to Godly Play*, Volume 2, by Jerome W. Berryman, Living the Good News, Denver, Colorado, 2002, ISBN 1 889108 96 0.) A pointer moves round, week by week, to show how the Church tells time. If your school is named after a saint, identify the saint's day on your clock.

Saints and special days

The celebration of the lives of saints forms part of the Anglican Church's calendar. Many of the saints, as well as showing inspiring qualities such as courage and humility, also proved to be lively characters with great stories to tell. Schools named after a saint can make a special celebration for their saint's day. For Christians, there is also the belief that everyone has the potential for holiness and so we are all saints in the making! A good time to celebrate this is All Saints' Day on 1 November, providing an appropriate alternative to Halloween.

Hymns and psalms

Hymns, like prayers, are a strong part of the Anglican tradition. The tradition is, however, very broad and draws on literary and musical styles, both historical and contemporary, from around the world. Use a mixture of long-established hymns and modern songs to complement the theme of an act of worship.

Psalms are a strong part of the Anglican tradition. Use a single verse, or sing them through a simple chant or hymn. Older pupils could read a short psalm antiphonally. Try Psalms 100, 121 or 150. Use them as inspiration to compose music or create a dance or mime.

Worldwide communion

The Anglican Church is a worldwide communion and a living and growing community of faith. Worship in Church schools can draw upon this rich and creative resource of music, literature and art. CMS and USPG produce excellent visual materials from all parts of the world, including colour postcards, overhead transparencies, and comprehensive notes. The resource pack called *Born Among Us* is a good resource for Advent and Christmas, and focuses on images from Africa and India. *The Christ We Share* is a collection of images of Jesus from Asia, Africa and South America. (See Resource list below, p. 146.)

Act of Worship 1
Three in One, One in Three

Introduction to the theme and its purpose

This act of worship introduces pupils to the Christian belief that there is one God who is known in three ways: God the Father, God the Son and God the Holy Spirit. Christians use symbols to illustrate this idea; symbols can so often say more than words.

Background

One of the distinctive features of Christianity is the central belief that God is revealed in three ways, God the Father, God the Son and God the Holy Spirit, yet remains one God. Early Christians tried to explain the mystery of this relationship by using the idea of the Trinity. The doctrine of the Trinity was defined in a statement of faith at the Council of Nicaea in AD 325. The Nicene Creed is still used today in Christian worship around the world. Christians are baptized in the name of the Holy Trinity. In the Christian calendar, Trinity Sunday marks the beginning of the Trinity season when the liturgical colour is green.

The American religious educator Jerome Berryman, in his book *The Complete Guide to Godly Play*, Volume 4 (2003), pp.136–42, suggests that the concept of the Trinity is a kind of 'three-in-one logic' that requires 'three-in-one-thinking'.

Preparation

- The worship leader needs to bring along three objects/pieces of clothing that represent three different aspects of their life.
- A focus table should be prepared, covered in a green cloth, with three candles and a Bible open at 2 Corinthians 13.
- An overhead transparency of the Trinity symbol on p. 122 may be used as a visual aid.

Suggested approach

Show the pupils the three artefacts you have brought along to illustrate three different roles in your life. Take each in turn and say:

This —— (name of object) tells you about Ms/Mr —— (your name) the —— (name of role).

For example: This packet of seeds tells you about Ms Smith the gardener.

Talk about each of the three aspects of your life and why they are part of what makes you the person you are.

Introduce the idea that these three roles are all different but you are still one person. That is the sort of idea that needs 'three-in-one thinking'!

Project the Trinity symbol on an overhead transparency.

Use the symbol and explore the idea that there are three distinct circles and they are all interconnected in one pattern. You will need some 'three-in-one thinking' to sort it out! How can one be three? How can three be one? How can things/people be the same but different?

For Christians, God is known as God the Father, God the Son and God the Holy Spirit; one God but three different ways of knowing God. This is the sort of mystery that needs 'three-in-one thinking'. Christians use symbols like this to help them think more about the mystery of the Trinity.

Turn off the overhead projector and shift your attention to the green focus table.

Reflection

Light the three candles on the focus table. As you do this, name the three ways in which Christians know God: God the Father, God the Son and God the Holy Spirit.

Have a short period of quietness before introducing the prayer.

Prayer/reading

When Christians meet together they often use this prayer. The words were first used by St Paul to end his Second Letter to the Corinthians (2 Corinthians 13.13). Listen to the 'three-in-one thinking' in the words of the prayer:

> The grace of the Lord Jesus Christ, the love of God, and the fellowship of the Holy
> Spirit be with you all.

Music

Sing the following verse, written by Bishop Thomas Ken (1637–1711), to the tune of Tallis's Canon.

> Praise God from whom all blessings flow,
> Praise him, all creatures here below,
> Praise him above, ye heavenly host,
> Praise Father, Son and Holy Ghost.

Other suggestions are:

'Halle, Halle, Hallelujah', or 'Glory to God' (also known as 'The Peruvian Gloria'). Both of these songs can be found in *Jump Up if You're Wearing Red*, The National Society/Church House Publishing,1996, ISBN 0 7151 4868 0.

Act of Worship 2
The Song of Mary

Introduction to the theme

This act of worship introduces pupils to the different ways in which Christians remember Mary, the Mother of Jesus. It focuses on the biblical account of when Mary is told by an angel that she will have a baby and this will be God's son. This event, called the Annunciation, is marked in the Christian calendar on 25 March. The act of worship also refers to the Song of Mary, the Magnificat, traditionally said, or sung, each day in the Evening Office.

Background

Mary, the Mother of Jesus, has always held a very important place in the Christian story. Different groups of Christians remember her in different ways and for different reasons, but she is revered as the Mother of God and there are several important feast days that mark key events in her life. Churches, cathedrals and places of pilgrimage around the world have been dedicated to her; your school may be one of many that bear her name. Considering her importance for Christians, there is very little information about her life in the Gospels. The story of the Annunciation and her song, the Magnificat, are significant references when trying to build a picture of the person of Mary.

Preparation

- Set up a focus table covered with a blue cloth. Place on it a Bible open at Luke's Gospel. Add some white flowers (traditionally lilies or roses are associated with Mary).

- Gather together pictures or figures of Mary, particularly images of the Annunciation. Christmas cards are a rich source of pictures created by artists around the world. Postcards and posters from art galleries are another source. The resource pack *Born Among Us* has images on overhead transparencies. Use the collection of images to make a display as a backdrop for your focus table.

- Prepare four large pieces of card. On the first write a large letter **M** on one side and on the reverse print the word 'messenger'. On the second write a large letter **A** on one side and on the reverse print the word 'awe'. On the third write a large letter **R** on one side and on the reverse print the word 'ready'. On the fourth write a large letter **Y** on one side and on the reverse print the word 'yes'.

- Make an overhead transparency of Mary's Song, on p. 123.

Reading

The Magnificat, also known as The Song of Mary, can be found in Luke 1.46–55. An adaptation has been written for this act of worship.

Suggested approach

Listen to a musical setting of the Magnificat as the pupils enter.

Explain that the music is called the Magnificat or The Song of Mary and introduce the theme for the act of worship: Mary, the Mother of Jesus and the most important Christian saint. Discuss with the pupils what they know or have heard about her: for example, from the Bible, from pictures, or from school Christmas plays. Start to build up a description of Mary using the pupils' ideas. Refer to the display of images and the focus table as stimuli for the discussion. Introduce the idea that artists have painted Mary in many different ways but she is often shown wearing blue – this was once the most expensive colour and so artists used it sparingly and only for their most precious work. Lilies are often included to symbolize Mary's purity.

The Bible does not tell us a great deal about Mary but St Luke, in his Gospel, tells us a very important story about her . . .

Introduce the pieces of card (see 'Preparation' above) and invite pupils to hold the cards, showing the four letters of Mary's name, for everyone to see. Retell the events of the Annunciation, taking one letter at a time and turning the card around to reveal the key words. Follow this scheme:

M – Messenger

The Bible is full of stories about angels being God's messengers. In this story, St Luke describes the Angel Gabriel coming to see Mary and telling her she is to have a very special baby.

A – Awe

Mary must have been full of awe and wonder when she heard the angel's amazing words. Gabriel said her child would be the Son of God and she was to call him Jesus.

R – Ready

Mary was very perplexed and wondered if she was ready to have a baby. The Angel Gabriel told Mary not to be afraid; she had been specially chosen by God to be the mother of Jesus.

Y – Yes

Mary listened to the words of the Angel and, before Gabriel disappeared, she agreed to do what God had asked of her. St Luke tells us that Mary sang about her joy of being chosen by God: she sang something like this . . .

Project the overhead transparency of Mary's Song. This could be read by one or more pupils.

Reverse the word cards again to show the letters of Mary's name.

Mary knew that the birth of her son, Jesus, would not just change her life but change the world. Mary, the mother of Jesus, has become the most important Christian saint. Every day, all around the world, Christians hear Mary's song and remember the time when Mary said 'Yes' to God.

Prayer

Light a candle on the focus table.

> Loving God,
> people are always asking us to do things;
> we have to make so many decisions:
> when to agree,
> when to say yes or no,
> when to believe,
> when to be the same or to be different.
> Be with us like you were with Mary.
> Help us to sort things out
> and find the best way to go.
> Amen.

Music

Magnificat, p. 104 in *Music from Taizé*, Collins Liturgical Publications, 1984.

(This simple chant can be sung as a round in two or more parts.)

There are many musical settings of the Magnificat available on CD: for example, Charles Stanford's Evening Service in C, *Stanford Sacred Choral Works*, Volume 3, Hyperion, 1999, CDA66974.

Act of Worship 3
Colours of the year

Introduction

This act of worship aims to give pupils the opportunity to think about the role and effect that colour has in their lives and the life of the Church. This material can be used as one act of worship or could be easily adapted into a series on the theme of colour. You could, for example, focus upon the colour of the current Church season, or look at one liturgical colour each day for a week.

Background

Colour is very powerful; it can evoke memories, represent a team, an event or a political viewpoint and can stir up emotions that cause us to stop and reflect. Throughout the year, colours and symbols are used to mark events in the Church calendar, to enrich worship, to aid reflection and to remind Christians of the Gospel story. Here is a brief summary:

Green is the colour most used in the Church year. It symbolizes a time of teaching, learning and growing.

Red is used during Holy Week and at Pentecost. It symbolizes the suffering of Jesus and the fire of the Holy Spirit.

Purple is used during the seasons of Advent and Lent. It symbolizes a time of waiting and preparation, a time when Christians say sorry to God.

White is used at Christmas and Easter. It symbolizes celebration, purity, hope and life.

Preparation

You will need:

- a piece of bright yellow card or paper;
- four pieces of card or paper in non-liturgical colours: for example, turquoise, orange, blue and brown;
- four pieces of cloth – one red, one white, one purple and one green – each large enough to drape across your focus table;
- to create an overhead transparency of p. 124 and have available an OHT pen in one of the liturgical colours.

Suggested approach

Begin with a sentence of welcome.

Leader	The Lord is here.
Response	**His Spirit is with us.**

We are surrounded by beautiful colours and they remind us of all sorts of things: different people, special times, food, games, natural objects, pictures, books. The colours can also have an effect upon our feelings and we like some colours more than others.

Show the pupils the piece of bright yellow card and ask them what the colour yellow reminds them of. They may give answers such as the sunshine, bananas or sand. Develop the discussion further by asking them how the colour yellow makes them feel and why it makes them feel that way. Share some reflections from your own experience: for example, you might say 'Yellow makes me feel excited because it reminds me of daffodils and the new growth of springtime.'

Explain that you are now going to show some more colours and for each one will ask the same two questions: 'What does the colour remind you of?' and 'How does the colour make you feel?' Go through your pieces of coloured paper at a reasonable pace, asking a few pupils each time to share their ideas.

Move on now to focus upon the four liturgical colours.

Project the picture of a church.

Explain that the Church has special colours, which it uses to remind us of the meaning behind the stories, special seasons and festival times. Ask 'I wonder if anyone knows the colours I am thinking of?' and 'I wonder if anyone has seen these colours in church?' as you carefully drape the pieces of coloured cloth across the focus table. As the children make suggestions, add colour to the picture of the church: for example, the altar frontal, the clergy vestments and lectern fall. Repeat the two questions about colours from earlier and encourage the children to reflect upon how the colours could be used in church. Ask questions like:

- I wonder how these colours could be used in church?
- I wonder why these colours are used in church?

Ask a member of staff to write down the children's comments and ideas. These could be used later to create a 'colour' display.

Reflection

Light a candle on the focus table.

Ask the pupils to sit very still and to think about the colours around them. Offer some wondering questions to guide their reflection:

- I wonder which colours you like best?
- I wonder which colours make you feel sad?
- I wonder which colours make you smile?

Prayer

Loving God,

We thank you for all the beautiful colours that you created for us to enjoy.

We thank you for colours that remind us of special times and special people;

for colours in church that remind us of you;

and we especially thank you for our favourite colours.

Amen.

Music

'Who put the colours in the rainbow?' in *Come and Praise 1*, BBC Education, 1978, ISBN 0 563 32067 2.

'Morning has broken' in *Come and Praise 1*, BBC Education, 1978, ISBN 0 563 32067 2.

'All things bright and beautiful' in *Junior Praise*, Marshall Pickering, ISBN 0 551 01293 5.

'Great is your faithfulness' in *Junior Praise*, Marshall Pickering, ISBN 0 551 01293 5.

The mystery of the Trinity needs some 3 in 1 thinking!

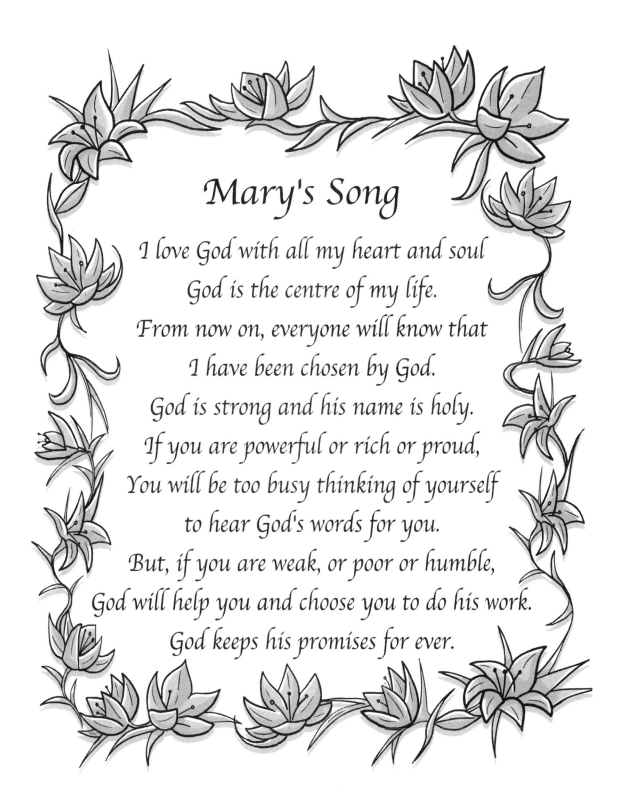

Mary's Song

I love God with all my heart and soul
God is the centre of my life.
From now on, everyone will know that
I have been chosen by God.
God is strong and his name is holy.
If you are powerful or rich or proud,
You will be too busy thinking of yourself
to hear God's words for you.
But, if you are weak, or poor or humble,
God will help you and choose you to do his work.
God keeps his promises for ever.

Be Anglican: OHT for Act of Worship 3

Something to think about

Be Anglican

Below is a list of elements of the Anglican heritage that can be drawn upon and used in school worship.

- The Bible as a source of inspiration and learning

- Christian symbols

- The cycle of seasons of the Anglican year

- A regular pattern of worship

- Responses, hymns and psalms

- Prayers, meditation and silence

- Music and the creative arts

Take each of these elements and decide how it can be incorporated in the worship programme.

What resources, including human resources, would be needed to develop your ideas?

In what way can your worship resource bank be developed to reflect the worldwide Anglican Church?

Be Structured: OHT Christian symbol – Chi Rho

9 Be Structured

Be Bold!

offers the challenge to
collective worship coordinators to . . .

be creative,

take risks,

try out new ideas.

Be Structured

is to help put this into action.

It provides a framework into which all the different
ingredients can go.

Be Structured: OHT for Training

Collective worship
is at the very
heart of daily life in
a Church school.

Collective worship at the heart of school life

Consider the place of collective worship in your school.

Use this statement (opposite page) as a starting point for discussion. Record responses and use these to evaluate the place of collective worship in your school.

Try using the 'heart' metaphor to explore the statement more deeply. For example:

- Is collective worship a life-giving experience – is it refreshing, tiring, enlivening, low on energy?

- Is collective worship the heartbeat of your school; is it a regular or irregular beat; is the pulse weak or strong?

- What is the impact of collective worship on the rest of the school day? Does it reach the parts other subjects don't reach?

- Is collective worship a safe place for pupils and staff to explore life issues; for religious commitment; to focus on God; to get to the heart of the matter?

- Does collective worship provide an opportunity for members of the school community to develop, however tentatively, their own personal relationship with God and discover God within their own heartbeat?

Some more direct, practical questions will also shed light on your considerations, for example:

- What is the status given to your daily act of worship?

- Is collective worship ever given priority on your school development plan?

- Is there a designated budget for collective worship resources and training?

Notes to accompany OHT

In collective worship in our school we aim to . . .

E xplore

E ncounter

E xperience

Explore, Encounter, Experience: aims for collective worship

Discuss what you would like pupils and staff to *explore*, *experience* and *encounter* in collective worship. The following points are offered to guide your discussion. Identify those with which you agree or disagree. Substitute examples of your own. Allow the distinctive nature of your school, and the people in it, to be reflected, then use the outcome to create aims for collective worship in your school policy.

Explore

- aspects of human experience which raise questions about the meaning and purpose of life;

- spiritual and moral issues;

- a reflective approach to religious and human issues;

- the part religion and faith play in history and in contemporary life;

- ideas about God and about a personal relationship with God;

- the teachings of the Bible and other religious texts;

- the place of values such as love, truth and goodness.

Encounter

- Christianity as a vibrant, contemporary and diverse tradition;

- Christianity in action, in creative silence and in the awe and wonder of the natural world;

- people of faith to demonstrate what it means to hold a religious view of life;

- worship and prayer as part of the natural rhythm of the day, rooted in an annual cycle of seasons and festivals;

- religious worship in an open, honest atmosphere;

- some of the diversity of Christian worship.

Experience

- a community where faith is taken seriously;

- being part of the school family; sharing the achievements, joys and challenges of all in the school community;

- a sense of awe, wonder and mystery;

- an atmosphere conducive to worship;

- worship that is enjoyable, creative and imaginative.

Notes to accompany OHT

Leading worship: Some guidelines

- Be **calm** and **organized**

- Include time for **thinking**
  sharing
  listening
  reflection

- Use a **focus**

- Make it **relevant**

- Make it **worshipful**

- **Be yourself**

Leading worship: Some guidelines

Always try to be **calm**; this is not the opposite of enthusiastic! Pupils quickly detect the difference between calm enthusiasm and panicking enthusiasm.

Aim to be **organized**. Be in the hall waiting for the pupils to arrive with props and focal materials at the ready. Ensure a sense of order when pupils enter and leave.

Thinking, **sharing**, **listening** and **reflection** are the basic ingredients of a quality act of worship. There is wisdom in the saying 'Less is more'. So keep it simple; it's easy to try to pack too much in to one act of worship.

Set up a **focus** table. Think of how to use colour, objects and images to capture the pupils' attention. Use religious artefacts, a candle, or an open Bible as a focus for worship.

As you prepare the act of worship, find ways of introducing a theme or an idea that will **capture the pupils' imagination**. Build bridges between their experience and the theme of the worship.

Create an atmosphere that is conducive to **worship**. Think about your body language, your attitude to pupils, and the tone and style of language you use. Is there a safe space for pupils to encounter God?

And finally, whether you are being bold, creative, still, thoughtful, humorous, multi-sensory, in Communion, Anglican, or structured, the most important thing is that you:

Be yourself.

Notes to accompany OHT

Planning a worship programme: a framework

Seasons, festivals and holy days

Beginnings and endings

Starting school

Moving on

Special days for your school

Be Structured: OHT for training

Planning a worship programme

When planning the themes for your school's annual worship programme, start with a framework for the year based on the following suggestions.

Seasons, festivals and holy days

Choose themes to reflect the pattern of the Church year. Mark in the Christmas Season (Advent, Christmas and Epiphany) and the Easter Season (Lent, Holy Week and Easter). Other major Christian festivals are Ascension, Pentecost, and All Saints' Day. There are also many other saints' days to choose from (see the list on p.138-9 for some ideas).

The Shap Working Party produces a calendar of religious festivals, giving dates of festivals for all the major world faiths. (Contact Shap on 020 7898 1494.)

Beginnings and endings

Choose themes to reflect the pattern of the school year. The start and end of term offer the opportunity for special gatherings.

Starting school

Note times when new pupils are starting school and offer a special collective worship to mark their arrival in the school community.

Moving on

Moving to a new class or changing school can be a significant rite of passage. Choose themes to explore the concept of 'change' and 'moving on' at these important times.

Special days for your school

If your school is named after an individual, place or significant event, choose a time to commemorate this. Many Church schools are named after saints, so the worship theme could mark the saint's day.

Once all this is in place, slot in themes for each week. The collective worship website, www.natsoc.org.uk (or www.culham.ac.uk), provides sample acts of worship for every week of the school year. And don't forget all the examples in each chapter of *Be Bold!*

Notes to accompany OHT

Planning sheet for an act of collective worship

Date...

Worship leader/s..

Theme...

**Introduction to the theme
and its purpose**

Background

Preparation

Suggested approach

Reading(s)

Prayer

Music

Feedback

Planning and recording an act of collective worship

The acts of collective worship in *Be Bold!* have been written using this outline. Use it to plan individual acts of worship or a series based on a particular theme. Keep the notes to create your own resource bank and as a tool for monitoring and recording collective worship in your school.

Introduction to the theme and its purpose

- Aims
- Setting and arrangement of space
- Year group/s

Background

- Knowledge/information useful to the worship leader
- Any resources for background reading

Preparation

- What you need to lead the worship
- Any preparation necessary for staff or pupils
- Focus table: colours, artefacts

Suggested approach

- Running order
- Useful things to say, questions to ask, styles of delivery

Reading(s)

- Reading from the Bible or other religious text, poem, quotation.

Prayer/reflection

- Words of the prayer or reference
- Use of silence
- Candle or other focus

Music

- For entering and leaving
- Hymns and songs

Feedback

- What worked or did not work
- Any feedback from pupils, colleagues, visitors
- What might you do differently next time?

Notes to accompany OHT

Calendar of festivals and holy days

The following table gives some of the principal feasts, holy days and festivals in the Church calendar. It also includes a number of the lesser festivals, commemorating the lives of popular saints. For a complete list of festivals and holy days, an essential reference is *Common Worship, Services and Prayers for the Church of England*, Church House Publishing, 2000. *Saints on Earth* (Church House Publishing, 2004) gives biographical information about each saint included in the *Common Worship* calendar.

Month	Date	Name
January	6	The Epiphany
	25	The Conversion of Paul
February	2	Candlemas
	*	Shrove Tuesday
	*	Ash Wednesday
March	1	David
	2	Chad
	17	Patrick
	19	Joseph of Nazareth
	20	Cuthbert
	25	The Annunciation
	*	Palm Sunday
	*	Maundy Thursday
	*	Good Friday
	*	Easter Day
April	23	George
	25	Mark
May	1	Philip and James
	14	Matthias
	31	Visit of the Blessed Virgin Mary to Elizabeth
	*	Ascension Day
	*	Pentecost
	*	Trinity Sunday
June	9	Columba
	11	Barnabas
	22	Alban
	24	The Birth of John the Baptist
	29	Peter and Paul

July	3	Thomas
	22	Mary Magdalene
	25	James
August	6	The Transfiguration
	15	The Blessed Virgin Mary
	24	Bartholomew
	31	Aidan
September	14	Holy Cross Day
	21	Matthew
	29	Michael and All Angels
October	4	Francis
	18	Luke
	28	Simon and Jude
November	1	All Saints
	11	Martin
	30	Andrew
	*	Advent Sunday
December	6	Nicholas
	25	Christmas Day
	26	Stephen
	27	John the Evangelist

* Variable dates

Seasonal colours in the Church year

Season	Colour
Advent	purple
Christmas	gold or white
Epiphany	gold or white
Candlemas	gold or white
Lent	purple
Holy Week	red
Easter	gold or white
Pentecost	red
Trinity	green
All Saints	gold or white
Kingdom	red

Christian symbols

Cross

The cross is Christianity's most important symbol, used by Christians throughout the world. The cross is used in different ways and has many meanings. A cross bearing the body of Jesus (crucifix) represents the appalling nature of Jesus' suffering and death. A plain cross is, for Christians, a powerful symbol of love and hope. The belief in Jesus' resurrection offers a joyous triumph over death and the promise of new life.

Fish

The fish is an ancient Christian symbol that pre-dates even the cross. It was used by the early Christians as a form of identification; a secret symbol used at a time when Christians were suffering persecution. The Greek word for fish is 'ichthus' and is an acronym of the Greek phrase *Iesous Christos Theou Uios Soter* – Jesus Christ, Son of God, Saviour.

Dove

The dove has come to have several meanings in Christian symbolism. In Christian art, a dove most commonly represents God the Holy Spirit (e.g. in images of the Annunciation, the Baptism of Jesus and the Holy Trinity). More generally, the dove is used a symbol of peace.

Gospel emblems

The symbols of the four Evangelists and their Gospels are often portrayed together: for example, in stained glass windows. St Matthew is usually represented by a figure of a man or angel; St Mark by a winged lion; St Luke by a bull or ox, again usually with wings; and St John by an eagle.

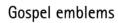

Star of creation

The six-pointed star is an ancient symbol of creation. It is also a reference to the Trinity. The three-sided, equilateral triangle represents the 'three in one' nature of the Trinity, Father, Son and Holy Spirit. In the star, the two triangles are interlinked.

Celtic cross

Celtic Christian artists used patterns with no apparent beginning or end to depict the belief that God's love is everlasting.

Bread and wine

Bread and wine (or wheat and grapes, or a chalice and paten) are used to symbolize the Last Supper and the Eucharistic meal. During the Last Supper, Jesus commanded his disciples to share bread and wine together, to remember him. Christians do this when they celebrate the Eucharist.

Paschal candle

A paschal candle is lit on Easter Day and each Sunday through the Easter Season. It is also lit for Baptisms. It is a large candle decorated with symbols of the life, death and resurrection of Jesus. Typically, it shows the letters alpha and omega, the first and last letters of the Greek alphabet. 'I am the Alpha and the Omega,' says the Lord God (Revelation 1.8).

Chi Rho

For Christians, Jesus is the Messiah, the Son of God, and the word Christ is used to identify him as such. The symbol is made up of the Greek letters X (chi) and P (rho), the first two letters of the Greek word for Christ (XPICTOC).

Appendix: Classic prayers in the Anglican tradition

We include here some classic prayers in the Anglican tradition. (Some of these were originally featured in the 'Anglican heritage' chapter of David Barton, Alan Brown and Erica Brown, *Open the Door*, Oxford Diocesan Education Services Ltd and The National Society, 1994). The Church of England's new *Common Worship* services also contain a rich treasury of prayer, which schools may wish to draw upon.

The Lord's Prayer

Our Father in heaven,
hallowed be your name,
your kingdom come,
your will be done,
on earth as in heaven.
Give us today our daily bread.
Forgive us our sins
as we forgive those who sin against us.
Lead us not into temptation
but deliver us from evil.
For the kingdom, the power and the glory are yours
now and for ever. Amen.

A prayer of St Patrick (adapted)

May the strength of God pilot us,
May the power of God preserve us,
May the wisdom of God instruct us,
May the hand of God protect us,
May the way of God direct us,
May the shield of God defend us.

May Christ be with us,
Christ above us
Christ in us
Christ before us
This day and evermore

A prayer attributed to St Francis of Assisi

Lord, make me an instrument of your peace:

Where there is hatred, let me sow love;

Where there is injury, pardon;

Where there is discord, union;

Where there is doubt, faith;

Where there is despair, hope;

Where there is darkness, light;

Where there is sadness, joy.

O divine Master,

grant that I may not so much seek to be consoled as to console;

to be understood as to understand;

to be loved as to love;

for it is in giving that we receive,

it is in pardoning that we are pardoned,

and it is in dying that we are born to eternal life.

From the prayer of St Richard of Chichester

O most merciful Redeemer, friend and brother:

may I know you more clearly,

love you more dearly,

and follow you more nearly, day by day.

A prayer of St Ignatius Loyola

Teach us, good Lord,

to serve you as you deserve;

to give and not to count the cost;

to fight and not to heed the wounds;

to toil and not to seek for rest;

to labour and not to seek for any reward,

save that of knowing that we do your will.

Psalm 23

The Lord is my shepherd, I shall not want.
He makes me lie down in green pastures;
he leads me beside still waters;
he restores my soul.
He leads me in right paths
for his name's sake.

Even though I walk through the darkest valley,
I fear no evil;
for you are with me;
your rod and your staff –
they comfort me.

You prepare a table before me
in the presence of my enemies;
you anoint my head with oil;
my cup overflows.
Surely goodness and mercy shall follow me
all the days of my life,
and I shall dwell in the house of the Lord
my whole life long.

Other Psalms you may wish to use: 121, 130, 150.

From the Holy Communion service

Almighty God,
to whom all hearts are open,
all desires known,
and from whom no secrets are hidden:
cleanse the thoughts of our hearts
by the inspiration of your Holy Spirit,
that we may perfectly love you,
and worthily magnify your holy name;
through Christ our Lord.
Amen.

A form of prayer for use in a classroom

The Iona Community in Scotland has, for many years, developed simple forms of prayer for use in small groups. What follows is a simple act of worship that could be used regularly in a class or tutor group.

Three candles or nightlights are needed, and these should be placed on a table where everyone can easily see them, perhaps with some flowers, a cross, or a natural object.

First leader   I will light a light
In the name of the Maker
Who lit the world
And breathed the breath of life for me.

A candle is lit and placed centrally

Second leader   I will light a light
In the name of the Son
Who saved the world
And stretched out his hand for me.

A candle is lit and placed centrally

Third leader   I will light a light
In the name of the Spirit
Who encircles the world
And blesses my soul with longing.

A candle is lit and placed centrally

All   We will light three lights
For the Trinity of love
God above us
God beside us
God beneath us
The beginning
The end
The everlasting one.

A moment of silence is kept.

Resources

Books, journals and poetry

Additional Collects, Church House Publishing, 2004.

Jerome W. Berryman, *The Complete Guide to Godly Play*, Living the Good News, Denver, Colorado, 2002-3.

    Vol. 1:   *How to Lead Godly Play Lessons,* ISBN 1 889108 95 2.

    Vol. 2:   *14 Presentations for Fall,* ISBN 1 889108 96 0.

    Vol. 3:   *17 Presentations for Winter,* ISBN 1 889108 97 9.

    Vol. 4:   *16 Presentations for Spring,* ISBN 1 889108 98 7.

    Vol. 5:   *Practical Help from Godly Play Trainers,* ISBN 1 931960 04 6.

J. W. Berryman, *Godly Play*, Augsburg, 1991, ISBN 0 8066 2785 9.

J. W. Berryman, *Teaching Godly Play*, Abingdon Press, 1995, ISBN 0 687 08651 5.

Alan Brown and Alison Seaman, *Encounter Christianity* Series, The National Society/Church House Publishing, 2001–2.

Key Stage One materials:

In Creation (Big Book)

In the Making

In Journeys

In Words

Key Stage Two materials:

To Change the World

In Journeys About Jesus

In Words About Jesus

In Questions About Jesus

Chelmsford Diocesan Resource Centre is an efficient supplier of Godly Play books.

    Tel.: 01245 294405

    Fax: 01245 294477

    Email: resources@chelmsford.anglican.org

Common Worship: Services and Prayers for the Church of England, Church House Publishing, 2000.

John Darch and Stuart Burns, *Saints on Earth*, Church House Publishing, 2004.

G. Dryden and J. Vos, *The Learning Revolution*, Accelerated Learning, 1994, ISBN 0 905553 43 8.

Sally Elton-Chalcraft, 'Empty Wells: how well are we doing at well-being?', *International Journal of Children's Spirituality*, Vol. 7, No. 3, 2002.

New Patterns for Worship, Church House Publishing, 2002.

Brendán Ó Madagáin, 'Cherish the earth', in *Cherish the Earth*, Mary Low (compiler), Wild Goose Publications, 2003, ISBN 1 901557 71 5.

Michael Perry (ed.), *The Dramatised Bible*, Marshall Pickering and Bible Society, 1989.

The Way Ahead: Church of England Schools in the New Millennium, Church House Publishing, 2001.

Calendars

The Shap Calendar of Religious Festivals
A colourful wallchart for display, accompanied by a booklet of explanatory notes and an A5 laminated diary card for quick reference. Festivals, dates and information for twelve major world religions. Price £5.20.

The Shap Pictorial Calendar 2005
Each month is illustrated with a photograph of a festival or religious event. It is accompanied by brief background information, cross-referenced with other Shap publications. The calendars are A4 size and offer a range of beautifully photographed images from around the world. Price £6.50 (including postage and packing).

If you would like to purchase either of these publications or require further information, contact:

>Mike Berry
>Shap
>PO Box 38580
>London SW1P 3XF
>Tel: 020 7898 1494
>Email: shap@natsoc.c-of-e.org.uk

Godly Play materials

Godly Play equipment may be ordered from St Michael's Cottage Crafts, a workshop for adults with disabilities. For a catalogue, contact:

>Bowthorpe Community Trust
>Bowthorpe Hall Road
>Norwich
>Tel.: 01603 746106

You can also make your own Godly Play equipment if you have someone who is good at woodwork who is prepared to help you.

www.godlyplay.com is the web site of a workshop in the United States where you can buy Godly Play equipment.

Online resources

Collective Worship Resource, Culham Institute in association with The National Society
at www.culham.ac.uk and www.natsoc.org.uk.

Encounter Christianity supporting resource material may be found at
www.encounterchristianity.co.uk.

Resource packs

Born Among Us resource pack, price £15, including postage and packing, is available from:

> USPG
> Partnership House
> 157 Waterloo Road
> London SE1 8UU
> Tel.: 020 7803 3413   Web: www.uspg.org.uk

The Christ We Share pack and CD-ROM, price £15 + £1.50 postage and packing, and the *A-cross the World* pack, price £15 + £1.50 postage and packing, are available from:

> The Marketing Assistant
> Church Mission Society
> Partnership House
> 157 Waterloo Road
> London SE1 8UU
> Tel.: 020 7803 3376   Email: sales@cms-uk.org

Putting the 'WOW' into Worship: Ideas and Resources for Collective Worship, Blackburn Diocese Board of Education and North Lancashire Methodist District. Available from:

> Blackburn Diocese Board of Education
> Church House
> Cathedral Close
> Blackburn BB1 5AA
> Tel.: 01254 54421 Ext. 240
> Price: £25 (including CD Rom) plus postage and packing.

Acknowledgements

The authors and publisher gratefully acknowledge permission to reproduce copyright material in this book. Every effort has been made to trace and contact copyright holders. If there are any inadvertent omissions we apologize to those concerned; please send any information to the publishers who will make a full acknowledgement in future editions.

All Scripture quotations are taken from The New Revised Standard Version of the Bible, Anglicized Edition (NRSV): copyright © 1989, 1995 by the Division of Christian Education of the National Council of the Churches of Christ in the United States of America.

The poem 'Creativity' (Chapter 2, Be Creative) is copyright © Breandán Ó Madagáin, published in *Cherish the Earth* by Mary Low, 2003, Wild Goose Publications, Glasgow G2 3DH, Scotland, and is reproduced by permission.

A prayer of St Ignatius of Loyola (Chapter 4, 'Be thoughtful' and the Appendix) is from, and a prayer attributed to St Patrick (Chapter 1, 'Be Bold') is adapted from, *Common Worship: Daily Prayer*, copyright © 2002, The Archbishops' Council.

The image of 'The Laughing Christ' (Chapter 5, 'Be Humorous') is published in The Christ We Share, produced jointly by USPG, CMS and the Methodist Church. USPG and CMS have made every effort to trace copyright and apologize to any copyright holder that they have been unable to trace.

The acts of worship 'Do Not Judge Too Quickly' and 'A Modern Parable' (Chapter 5, 'Be Humorous') were inspired by outlines in *Assembly Point*, published by Scripture Union but no longer in print.

The act of worship 'A Harvest Rainbow' (Chapter 6, 'Be Multi-sensory') was inspired by 'Celebrating Harvest: God in All Things' in *Times and Seasons*, published jointly by Christians Aware and the Westminster Diocese Education Service, 1999, ISBN 1-873372-09-4 (available from Christians Aware, Tel. 0116 254 0770).

The act of worship 'A Journey through Holy Week' (Chapter 6, 'Be Multi-sensory') was devised by Lilian Weatherley, Trudie Bateman and Trevor Reader for primary schools in the Diocese of Winchester.

The Eucharistic prayer and the dismissal (Chapter 7, 'Be in Communion'), the greeting (Chapter 8, 'Be Anglican'), The Lord's Prayer and the Prayer of Preparation from the Holy Communion service (Appendix), are from *Common Worship: Services and Prayers for the Church of England*, copyright © 2000, The Archbishops' Council.

The Kyrie confessions, the absolution and the post communion prayer (Chapter 7, 'Be in Communion') are from *New Patterns for Worship*, copyright © 2002, The Archbishops' Council.

The School Eucharist checklist (Chapter 7, 'Be in Communion') was devised by the Revd Richard Harper.

The materials in Chapter 9, 'Be Structured', were inspired by *Putting the 'WOW' into Worship: Ideas and Resources for Collective Worship*, Blackburn Diocesan Board of Education and North Lancashire Methodist District.

A prayer of St Patrick (adapted) in the Appendix is from *A Celtic Evening Liturgy*, copyright © The Iona Community, Wild Goose Publications, Glasgow G2 3DH, Scotland.

The prayer beginning 'I will light a light' in the Appendix is from *A Wee Worship Book* (Wild Goose Publications, 1999) copyright © WGRG, Iona Community, G2 3DH.

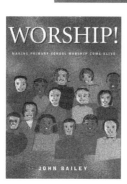